Richard Warner

An Illustration of the Roman Antiquities Discovered at Bath

Richard Warner

An Illustration of the Roman Antiquities Discovered at Bath

ISBN/EAN: 9783337020187

Printed in Europe, USA, Canada, Australia, Japan

Cover: Foto ©ninafisch / pixelio.de

More available books at **www.hansebooks.com**

AN

ILLUSTRATION

OF THE

Roman Antiquities

DISCOVERED AT

BATH.

By the Rev. RICHARD WARNER,
CURATE OF St. JAMES's PARISH.

FVIMVS

PUBLISHED BY ORDER
OF THE MAYOR AND CORPORATION.

BATH: PRINTED BY W. M.

TO THE RIGHT WORSHIPFUL

THE MAYOR, ALDERMEN, AND CHIEF CITIZENS

OF

BATH,

THE FOLLOWING ILLUSTRATION OF CERTAIN

ROMAN ANTIQUITIES,

ORIGINALLY DISCOVERED,

AND BY THEIR CARE AND ATTENTION,

NOW PRESERVED IN

𝕿𝖍𝖆𝖙 𝕮𝖎𝖙𝖞,

IS RESPECTFULLY INSCRIBED

BY THEIR OBEDIENT,

HUMBLE SERVANT,

BATH, FEB. 13,
179.

RICHARD WARNER.

INTRODUCTION.

WERE we to give credit to the fanciful defcriptions of Jeffery of Monmouth, and other fabling affertors of the Britifh antiquities, we fhould believe, that the arts and fciences, the elegancies, luxuries, and refinements of life, were known and practifed by the Britons, long before their communication with the Romans; and we might be perfuaded, that even Bath itfelf made a confiderable figure, as a city, fome centuries previous to the Chriftian Æra.¹ But if we turn from thefe wild dreams of the cloifter, to the page of claffical hiftory, we fhall find (from the few hints on the fubject which may there be met with) that

¹ Little, if any, credit can be given to the details of Britifh tranfactions previous to the arrival of the Romans here, as Polydore Virgil hath well obferved. Equidem nihil occultius; nihil incertius; nihil ignoratius; rebus Britannorum a principio geftis; partim quod annales, fi qui fuerant, ficut fupra oftendimus Gildam teftificari, funditus perierant, unde poftea qui hiftorias fcripferunt, nihil haurire potuere, &c. Hift. p. 18, l. 21.

the

the original inhabitants of our country little deferved
the fplendid character thus attributed to them. Scarcely
emerged from thofe fimple modes of life which are denominated the *hunter ftate*, the Britons, when firft difcovered
by the Romans, did not by any means prefent a picture
of national refinement. It was only near the coaft [1] that
any traces of civilization appeared; and for this partial
improvement in manners, the inhabitants were indebted
to the communication which they maintained with the
continental nations, through the medium of commerce.
In the interior parts of the country all was wild and favage.
Towns there were none;[2] the fcattered dwellings of the
natives were but miferable huts,[3] and many of the moft
obvious comforts and conveniences of life were utterly
unknown to them. Warlike and fierce,[4] but at the fame
time mild and merciful;[5] precipitate and inconftant,[6] but
generous and candid;[7] proud and haughty,[8] but benevo-
lent and hofpitable;[9] the ancient Britons exhibit, in the
page of hiftory, that inconfiftent character which is only

---

1 Cæfar fpeaking of the Belgic Britons, fays, " Ex his omnibus longe humaniffimi
" funt qui Cantium incolunt; quæ regio eft maritima omnis: neque multum a Gal-
" lica differunt confuetudine." Cæs. Bel. Gal. lib. 5.

2 Dion. Cafs. Lib. 39.

3 Diod. Sic. L., 5. c. 8.

4 Herodian lib. 3.

5 Hofpitibus boni mitefque fupplicibus. Pomp. Mela. lib. 3.

6 Rumoribus atque auditionibus permoti de fummis fæpe rebus confilia ineunt.
Cæs. Bel. Gal. lib. 4.

7 Diod. Sic. lib. 5.

8 Celtæ magna de feipfis fentiunt. Arrian. Exped. Alex,

9 Diod. Sic. lib. 5.

found

found in an early stage of society, when men unacquainted with the obligations and ties of morality or religion, regulate their conduct, not by any fixed principles, but by the wild impulse of the passions, or the whimsical dictates of caprice.

This consideration alone is sufficient to overturn the imaginary system of old British refinement, which the writers above alluded to, in a mistaken regard for the honor of their country, have endeavoured to foist upon us; and convinces us, that if we expect to discover any trait of it previous to the arrival of the Romans in this kingdom, our hopes will be altogether disappointed.

Confining our attention therefore to the period subsequent to this event, we shall endeavour to throw some light on the History of Bath, under the conquerors of the world; to whom we are indebted for the remains of ancient art, which it is the purpose of the following sheets to illustrate.

Fifty-five years before the birth of our Saviour, Julius Cæsar discovered Britain to the Roman world.¹ I say discovered, because his partial penetration into it, and his contests with two or three tribes of the natives, scarcely

1 Primus omnium Romanorum Divus Julius cum exercitu Britanniam ingressus, Tacit, Vit, Agric. C. 13.

amount

amount to any thing further.¹ The *conquest* of the country
did not take place till nearly a century afterwards. The
long and bloody civil wars in which contending ambition
plunged the Republic, kept, for a confiderable time, the
attention of the divided Romans confined to themfelves—
When, at length, the fiercenefs of party was quieted, and
the commonwealth overturned by the fuperior addrefs and
good fortune of Auguftus; the Emperor, fully employed
in reconciling the minds of the Romans to this new fpecies
of domination, had neither time nor inclination to attend
to the conquelt of a diftant nation, barbarous and wild,
and cut off as it were from all the habitable world.² Tiberius imitated the politic conduct of Auguftus in this
refpect; and all the preparations of the weak, wicked, and
capricious Caligula evaporated in folly. Nor was it till
the reign of Claudius, about the year of our Lord 44,
that any part of Britain was fairly reduced under the
Roman yoke; when Flavius Vefpafian carried the eagle
in triumph through the Belgic provinces, and compleatly
fubdued all the weftern, and fouth-weftern parts of
Britain.³

---

1 Quamquam profpera pugna terruerit incolas, ac litore potitus fit, poteft videri
oftendiffe pofleris, non tradidiffe. Ibid.   Intactus aut Britannus, Flor. Epod. 7. v. 7.

2 Et penitus toto divifos orbe Britannos.   Virgil. Ec. 1. v. 67.

3. Mox bella civilia, et in rempublicam verfa principum arma, ac longa oblivio
Britanniæ etiam in pace. Confilium id divus Auguftus vocabat, Tiberius præcep-
tum. Agitaffe C. Cæfarem de intranda Britannia fatis conftat, ni velox ingenio,
mobilis pœnitentia, et ingentes adverfos Germaniam conatus fruftra fuiffent. Divus
Claudius Auctor Operis, tranfvectis legionibus auxiliifque, et affumpto in partem
rerum Vefpafiano, quod initium venturæ mox fortunæ fuit, domitæ gentes, capti
reges, et monftratus fatis Vefpafianus, Tacit. in Vit. Agric. c. 13.

To

To this period then we are to look for the origin of Bath.¹— No sooner had the Romans penetrated into this part of Somersetshire, than the warm and medicinal springs, which had, probably, hitherto flowed unattended to along the vale, caught their observation, and quickly determined them to erect a station on the spot. Habituated as they were to the use of the bath, they gladly availed themselves of a situation which promised them, with little trouble, the indulgence that could not be procured in their own country without great labour and expence; and considering this advantage as fully counterbalancing all inconveniencies, they were content to forego their usual principles in choice of situation, and instead of fixing on any of the neighbouring commanding hills for their residence, they planted a colony on the scite of present Bath, in the hollow bottom of a deep and close valley.

The legions which accompanied Vespasian to England were the 2d, the 9th, the 14th, and the 20th. These, as the Romans extended themselves in the county, were dispersed through the stations that marked their line of conquest. Part of them of course remained at Bath, to

---

1 The country around Bath might have been conquered by *Osorius*, and the colony of *Aquæ Solis* established by him.—He subdued the *Iceni* and *Cangi*, (a people of this part of Somersetshire) about the year of our Lord 50, and built a regular chain of forts upon the banks of the severn and Avon. Many of his *castra æstiva*, or *exploratoria* are still plainly discernible. Compare Tacit. Annal. lib. xii. c. 31. " *Osorius detrahere arma suspectis, cin iofque castris Sabrinum et Antinam fluvios cohibere parat.*" A notification of Osorius's presence in these parts, is met with in the name of *Axe* passage, called in Doomsday-book Oster-clive, an evident corruption of the Roman appellation Osorius.

regulate

regulate and keep quiet the newly acquired territory. A detachment of the fecond legion was appointed to this fervice; the foldiers of which immediately employed themfelves in clearing the country around, and erecting proper barracks and refidences for the accommodation of the Cohort. The place was then eftablifhed into a colony;[1] and the name of *Aquæ Solis*,[2] or waters of the Sun, impofed

---

1 Fuerint olim apud Brittones xcii urbes, earum vero celebriores, et præ reliquiis confpicuæ xxxiii. Municipia fcilicet 11 ; Verolamium et Eboracum ; viiii coloniæ fc. Londinium, Augufta. Camalodunum, Geminæ Martiæ—Rhutupis. Thermæ —Aquæ Solis—Ifca Secunda—Deva Getica—Glevum, Claudia—Lindum—Camboricum—Ricardi Corinenfis de fitu Brit. c. vii. The colonies were fubject to the Roman Laws; enjoyed all the rights of Roman citizens ; and were governed by a fenate of their own election. Coloniæ—jura conftitutaque omnia populi Romani habent. Aulus Gel. Noct. Att. lib. xiv. c. 31.

2 Aquæ Solis is the name of Bath in the Itinerary of Antoninus ; where it occurs thus—" Iter xiv. Item alio Itinere ab Ifca (Carleon) Callevam (Ilchefter) M. P. ciii. (103 miles).

Ab Ifca - - - -	- -	From Caerleon.
Venta Silurum - -	M. P. ix. - -	Caergwent.
Abone - - - -	M. P. iv. - -	Aunfbury.
Trajectus - - - -	M. P. ix. - -	Henhùm
Aquis Solis - - -	M. P. vi. - -	Bath.

In *Ptolemy's geography* Bath occurs under the name of Ὕδατα θιρμα, or warm waters. Τοις δε Δοβινοι; ΒΕΑΓΑΙ κ πολεις. Ισχαλις (Ifca) Ὕδατα θιρμα (Bath) Οιιντα (Venta). The βαδιζα mentioned by Stephanus from Polybius is fuppofed to have been another name for the fame city. ΒΑΔΙΖΑ, πολις της Βρετλανιας, Πελυβιος τρισκαιδεκατω, το εθνικον ΒαδιζαιϾ. Step: de Urb: Tho' Wefeling doubts, and with good reafon, whether it were intended under that name. Imo facile reperias qui Βαδιζα Polybii apud Steph: huc referant, impulfi, ut liquet, recentiore Aquarum nomine Bath ; quod ipfum fi Britannis Polybii ætate ufitatum fuiffe commonftrarent nondum rem tenerent : neque enim ufque a Polybio fcriptum accepimus in ea urbe calidarum aquarum balinea fuiffe. *Bathonia* prava Latinitate Ofbernus in Vit. S. Elphegi c. 1. appellat—Wefeling. Anton. Itin. p. 486.

upon

upon it; in allufion to its warm medicinal fprings, which were fuppofed to receive their heat from the influence of that vivifying planet.

Having arranged thefe neceffary preliminaries, the next care of the Romans was to collect together the mineral waters that had hitherto walled their healing powers on the wild folitudes through which they flowed; and to erect baths for the pleafure, health, and comfort of the inhabitants of the new city.

This we are juftified in fuppofing would be a very early ftep with the Romans after their fettlement here; fince there was no luxury in higher eftimation with them than frequent bathing. As linen was not generally ufed till the times of the lower empire, cleanlinefs rendered conftant ablutions abfolutely neceffary; and, hence it was (according to an ancient writer), that the decent Roman, after every fort of exercife, or corporal exertion, plunged into the Bath, to free himfelf from the difagreeable confequences of extreme heat, and to refrefh and invigorate his exhaufted frame.[1] The like indulgence was generally ufed immediately before fupper, the great meal of this luxurious people;[2] though fome adopted a contrary prac-

---

1 Αλλα τ πολιμοι καταρ;νψ τμινο' τ μιγαλα παυσαμιοι πουλωιτο. Artimid: Daldian: Oneir: Lib: 1. c. 66.

2 Pro hinc cubiculo te refer, et lectulo laffitudinem refove, et ex arbitrio lavacrum pete nos quarum voces accipis, tuæ famulæ, fedulò tibi præminiftrabimus, nec corporis curatæ tibi regales epulæ morabuntur. L: Apul: Metam: Lib: 5. in princip:

tice,

tice, and never bathed till afterwards.¹ Whatever difference, however, there might be in the times of using them, the baths were places of great refort, and crouded with every defcription of character—the fenfual and the wife; the idle and the active; the fpendthrift and the mifer; the philofo-pher and the buffoon.—Here, not only the body of the bather was refrefhed by every art of wafhing, anointing,² rubbing, pinching, fqueezing, &c.³ but his eye was amufed with the fight of gymnaftic exercifes, in the furrounding Xyfti and porticoes; and his ear gratified with the recita-tion of poems, fongs, and various other compofitions, which the authors, for the gratification of their vanity, or for the fale of their works, were wont to repeat to the company affembled at the Baths.

To provide for a practice that contributed fo greatly to comfort us well as amufement, and which conftant habit had rendered altogether neceffary to the Romans, would occupy their immediate attention, after having difpatched the more important concerns of their new colony; and it is probable thofe remains of fplendid baths, difcovered in the year 1755, were part of the original *Thermæ* erected at

---

1 Οἱ δὲ ιμφαγοντες, ατα δι λυοιται. Artim. ut fupra.

2 The luxurious Roman went to a confiderable expence both in the ointments ufed on thefe occafions, and the materials with which his body was rubbed after their application. Jam Trimalcio unguento tergebatur non linteis, fed palliis ex molliffi-ma lana factis. Petron: Arb. in Satyr: p. 21.

3 Scabor, fuppellor, defquamor, pumicor, ornor,
  Expilor, pingor—Says a bather in Lucilius.

Aquæ

Aquæ Solis, as foon as the conquerors were once fettled in that place.¹

The following defcription of thefe remains is extracted from the Hiftory of Somerfetfhire; an account which I deemed it neceffary to introduce, as they are now entirely hidden from infpection, by buildings erected over them.

" The walls of thefe baths were eight feet in height, built
" of wrought ftone lined with a ftrong cement of terras;
" one of them was of a femicircular form, fifteen feet in
" diameter, with a ftone feat round it eighteen inches high,
" and floored with very fmooth flag ftones. The defcent
" into it was by feven ftone fteps, and a fmall channel for
" conveying the water ran along the bottom, turning at a
" right angle towards the prefent King's Bath. At a fmall
" diftance from this was a very large oblong bath, having
" on three fides a colonade, furrounded with fmall pilaflers,
" which were probably intended to fupport a roof. On
" one fide of this bath, were two fudatories nearly fquare,
" the floors of which were compofed of brick, covered
" with a ftrong coat of terras, and fupported by pillars of
" brick, each brick being nine inches fquare, and two inches
" in thicknefs. Thefe pillars were four feet and a half high,
" and fet about fourteen inches afunder, compofing a
" Hypocauft, or vault for the purpofe of retaining the

---

1 They were certainly among the *firft* of the Roman works here, being difcovered at the depth of *twenty feet* below the furface of the ground'; which is four feet lower than any of the other, and probably later fragments of architecture were found.

" heat

" heat neceffary for the rooms above. The interior walls
" of thefe apartments were fet round with tubulated bricks
" or funnels, about eighteen inches long, with a fmall
" orifice opening inwards, by which the fteam of heat was
" communicated to the apartment. The fire-place from
" which the heat was conveyed was compofed of a fmall
" conical arch at a little diflance from the outward wall;
" and on each fide of it, adjoining to the above-mentioned
" rooms, were two other fmaller fudatories of a circular
" fhape, with feveral fmall fquare baths, and a variety of
" apartments which the Romans ufed preparatory to their
" entering either the hot baths or fudatories; fuch as the *Fri-*
" *gidarium,* where the bathers undreffed themfelves, which
" was not heated at all; the *Tepidarium* which was mode-
" rately heated, and the *Eleothefion,* which was a fmall room,
" containing oil, ointments, and perfumes. Thefe rooms
" had a communication with each other, and fome of them
" were paved with flag ftones, and others beautifully teffel-
" lated with fmall dies of various colours. A regular fet of
" well-wrought channels conveyed the fuperfluous water
" from thefe baths to the river Avon."

The new colony being thus furnifhed with magnificent
baths, which were found to be not only pleafurable, but
(from the quality of their fprings) extremely healthy alfo
to thofe who ufed them, foon became a place of refort.
The Roman enervated by luxury, or worn out with toil,

‡ M. Vitruvius, lib: **8. c. 2.**

fought

fought strength and renovation in thofe very ftreams which
give health and energy to the difabled of the prefent day;
and our Britifh anceftors themfelves, quitting, by degrees,
the wild receffes of the neighbouring forefts, and the
rudeneffes of favage life, would at length be brought to
admire the elegancies, and participate in the delights of
Aquæ Solis.[1]

A progreffive improvement in the number and magni-
ficence of the buildings, and a gradual increafe in wealth and
population, would be the natural confequences of this univerfal refort to the waters of the fun.—Exclufive, however,
of the celebrity which the virtues of its fprings conferred
on the place; it received an addition of refpeftability from
its being the fituation of a *mint*; and the only town in this
part of Britain for the manufafture of the legionary arms.
The former affertion is rendered probable, from the circumftance of Bath being one of the nine colonies that the
Romans eftablifhed in Britain; which colonies, as well as
the two municipia, were indulged with the privilege of
minting their own coin. The faft of the great military
forge being eftablifhed at the fame place, will be found to
be proved by the obfervations on the firft fepulchral monument confidered in the following fheets.

1 Paullatinque disceffum ad delinimenta vitiorum, porticus, et balnea, et conviviorum elegantiam: idque apud imperitos humanitas vocabatur. Tacit: Agric;
Vit: c. 21.

The

The Roman city when compleated, exhibited a pentagon in form; of twelve hundred feet in length, and about eleven hundred feet in breadth, at the widest part. A strong wall nine feet thick, and twenty in height surrounded it. Five circular towers, one at each angle, defended this wall; and four gateways, which, according to the Roman principle, faced the cardinal points, gave entrance into the city The fosse-road, one of the four great British military ways, ran immediately through it from North to South, and was intersected at right angles, by another street, running in a direction East and West. In the centre of the city, (the scite of the present Abbey church-yard, and the upper part of Stall-street) were situated the Prætorium; the residences of the centurions, and military tribunes; together with the spacious baths, and a magnificent temple dedicated to Minerva.[1] Whilst various other temples, sacella, votive altars, and consecrated statues, were dispersed in other parts, and gave additional splendor to *Aquæ Solis.*

It is probable the far greater part of its inhabitants, at least for a considerable time after the establishment of the colony, consisted of legionaries; as the Romans do not

[1] Many parts of this temple are still preserved, which attest its former elegance, and place its erection at an early period of the Roman dominion in this country. Amongst them are a beautiful Corinthian capital, and an elegant fragment of cornice, equally excellent in their design and execution; and several pieces of columns, architraves, and friezes.—Most of these point at the *Corinthian* order, and lead to the conclusion, that this temple of Minerva was originally of that style of architecture; the only example of it (according to the observation of Mr. Burke, when he saw the remains) as yet discovered in Britain,

appear

appear to have allowed many of the natives to incorporate with them in their settlements of this nature.¹ But at the same time, it cannot be questioned, that some of the Britons would at length, from various causes, be drawn thither; and assist in forming that considerable population which the great extent of the original city proves it to have formerly boasted.

About the year of our Lord 72 or 73, Julius Agricola, whose character and actions have been so admirably detailed by the incomparable Tacitus, was appointed Legate of Britain, by the Emperor Vespasian. It was fortunate for the Roman interests in this country, that a commander so able and vigilant should be named to the regulation of their affairs here; for although their dominion had been but of a few years continuance, yet a sad relaxation in military discipline, and a carelessness and profligacy of manners, had already crept in, which rendered them despicable in the eyes, and open to the attacks of the surrounding Britons. The activity, vigilance, and superior talents of the new propraetor, quickly restored respectability to the Roman arms, and order and discipline amongst the legionaries.

1 We may infer this from the account Tacitus gives of the *general slaughter* committed by the Britons upon the inhabitants of Verulam, Colchester, and London (the two latter of which were *colonies*), under Bonduca's revolt; a destruction that would have been less universal, had these places been inhabited, in any considerable proportion, by their own countrymen.—Compare Tacit, Annal: lib. 14. c. 33.

The

The *Silures* and *Ordovices* (inhabitants of Wales), were yet unfubdued; and being a warlike and hardy people, offered a noble harveft of glory to the gallant mind of Agricola. He accordingly bent his attention to that quarter, and in a fhort time compleatly conquered the whole of Wales, and all its neighbouring ifles. But the talents of Agricola were not only fuch as fhone with unrivalled luftre in the field of battle—he was equally qualified to conquer, and to fecure his acquifitions by the moft falutary political regulations. — Intimately acquainted with human nature, he was aware, that whilft the Roman dominion over the Britons was fupported by the principle of fear alone, it would be but precarious and infecure.—He faw that their minds as well as bodies muft be fubdued, that it was neceffary to wean them from their old habits, manners, and modes of thinking, which had all a tendency to keep alive a warm fpirit of national pride and courage, and an ardent thirft for liberty, utterly incompatible with fyftematic fubjection.—No fooner had the rigour of winter precluded further military operations therefore, than he directed his attention to the execution of a plan, conceived in the very fpirit of political wifdom. The difperfed and uncivilized Britons were called together, and encouraged both by precept and example, to imitate the focial habits of Roman life. All the neceffary arts were firft communicated to them; afterwards fuch as are more immediately connected with comfort and elegance. They were inftructed in Roman literature; taught to admire and imitate Roman architecture; to adopt the Roman garb; to affect

Roman

Roman manners; to practice all the modifications of Roman luxury; and thus, under the fair shew of civilization and refinement, to emasculate their minds; extinguish their native dignity of spirit; and fit themselves for uncomplaining servitude, and irreversible bondage.[1]

As the expeditions of Agricola had been hitherto confined to Wales, and its neighbourhood, there is no doubt that part of his army would, during this period, be occasionally at Aquæ Solis; and it is equally probable, this colony would be the chief theatre on which these political arts of the sagacious commander were displayed.

In the year of our Lord 120 the Emperor Hadrian crossed to England, accompanied by the sixth legion. A cohort of this body seems to have been settled at Bath soon after its arrival; as may be inferred from the style of the letters, the nature of the ligatures, and other circumstances in the inscriptions No. 5, and No. 6, which commemorate an officer of this legion, and appear to claim an antiquity as high as the middle of the second century.

---

1 Sequens Hiems saluberrimis confiliis abfumpta. Namque ut Homines difperfi ac rudes, *eoque bella faciles, quieti et otio per voluptates affuefcerent:* hortari privatim, adjuvare publice, ut templa, foca, domus exftruerent, laudando promptos, et caftigando fegnes—Ita honoris æmulatio, pro neceffitate erat. Jam vero principum filios liberalibus artibus erudire, et ingenia Britannorum ftudiis Gallorum anteferre, ut qui modo linguam Romanam abnuebant, eloquentiam concupifcerent. Inde etiam habitus noftri honor, et frequens toga. Paullatimque difceffum ad delinimenta vitiorum, porticus, et balnea, et conviviorum elegantiam. *Idque apud imperitos humanitas vocabatur. cum pars fervitutis effet.* Tacit· in Vit: Agric. c. 21. Edit: Elzi. 1665.

Similar

Similar authorities evince that part of the twentieth legion, and a proportion of the Vettonenfian horfe, were quartered at the fame place,[1] but when flationed, or how long they continued at Bath, it is impoffible to fay. The latter not being mentioned in the *Notitia Imperii*, (which furvey was drawn up a little previous to the middle of the fifth century) had moft likely quitted the ifland before that time.—Of the former we can glean no information; fince the only mention made of them in this country, is contained in our infcription No. 2, and in another found at Bowes in Yorkfhire, and preferved by Horfley.[2]

Towards the commencement of the fifth century, the Romans, being extremely preffed by the incurfions of the Gothic nations, found it neceffary to withdraw their forces from the diftant provinces, in order to defend the heart of the empire ; and Britain, of courfe, amongft their other dependencies, was obliged to render up a proportion of her legionaries. Upwards of twenty thoufand Roman foldiers, were, however, ftill left in the kingdom, and remained there for twenty-five, or thirty years after the firft requifition.—But the exigencies of the empire becoming ftill more preffing, even thefe were at length recalled ; and all the legioraries finally left Britain about the middle of the fifth century, in the reign of Theodofius the fecond.

1 Vide No. 1, and No. 2.

2 The infcription runs thus : *Deæ Fortunæ Virius Lupus Legatus Auguftalis proprætor balineum vi ignis exuftum cohors prima Thracum reftituit curante Valerio Frontone præfecto equitum alæ Vettonum.* Brit : Rom : Infcrip : Yorkfhire, No. 1.

Then

Then probably, and not till then, would the Roman inhabitants of Aquæ Solis, reluctantly quit their abodes, and relinquish to the Britons, a city originally raised by Roman labour; decorated by Roman taste; and offering to the voluptuary all the arts of Roman diffipation.

Such is the amount of the fcanty and imperfect information which we have been able to collect, relative to the Roman hiftory of Bath.—The numerous remains of claffical architecture, however, which have been at various times difcovered here, prove, beyond a doubt, that it muft have been a magnificent city, in which the fine arts flourifhed, and were liberally cultivated. The Romans, blending a tafte for thefe, with their paffion for dominion, made fome amends for their devaftations, by immediately adorning what they conquered: and concealing the veftiges of havoc, under the nobleft monuments of architecture. Many of the fragments dug up at Bath, are in a ftyle of elegant mafonry that marks the æra of their execution to have been during the firft century, before the arts were much paft their zenith in Rome; moft of them, however, are of later date, and were probably executed after the third century, when the arts had fadly degenerated in the weftern world, owing to the building of Conftantinople, and the various irruptions and depredations of the uncivilized Northern nations on the Roman empire.

A confiderable number of fragments, and feveral imperfect infcriptions, exclufive of thofe illuftrated in the

D following

following pages, have been difcovered in, and immediately near the city of Bath, at different times.— Many
of thefe are not now to be found, and feveral which remain,
are fo mutilated as not to admit any conjecture relative to
their original defignation.[1] It may, however, be gratifying
to the reader to be informed what the infcriptions were ; I
fhall therefore conclude this introduction with a few ex-
tracts from Leland, Camden, Guidott, and Horfley, that
will afford a general account of them.

John Leland, the antiquary, was authorized by Henry
the Eighth, in the 25th year of his reign, to make a tour
through the kingdom for the purpofe of inveftigating the
national antiquities, more particularly the monaftic ones,
and collecting charters, deeds, records, manufcripts, &c.
from the libraries of the different religious houfes.   It was

[1] There is one exception to this. In the year 1790, two fragments were dug up,
in preparing an excavation for the foundation of the new Pump-room, bearing part
of an infcription, cut in fharp and elegant Roman capitals. Puzzling as the letters
are in their prefent flate, Governor Pownal has, with infinite ingenuity, and great
learning, enucleated their meaning, and recovered the infcription of which they
make a part.—He reads it, with the greateft probability, as follows ; and fuppofes it
to have been placed in the frieze of an entablature, of a portico, belonging to the
Ædis Salutis, at _Aquæ Solis_.

AULUS CLAUDIUS LIGURIUS SODALIS ASCITUS FABRORUM COLLEGIO
LONGA SERIA DEFOSSA HANC ÆDEM E NIMIA VETUSTATE LABENTEM DE IN-
VENTA ILLIC PECUNIA REFECI ET REPINGI CURAVIT.

The import of which is ; A : C : Ligurius a member of the College of the Fabri, or
armourers, refitted and beautified, (from a fum of money found in a _feria_ or earthen
veffel) the _Ædes Salutis_, or Temple of Health, which was in a ruinous flate.
Gov. Pownal's defcription, &c. of Bath Antiquities, p. 11, et infra.

during

during this progrefs that he vifited Bath, where he found the following fragments of Roman mafonry.

" There be divers notable antiquities engraved in ftone,
" that yet be fene yn the walles of Bathe betwixt the South
" gate and the Welle gate; and agayn betwixt the Welle
" gate and the North gate.

" The firft was an antique hed of a man made al flat,
" and having great lokkes of here as I have in a coine of
" C. Antius.

" The fecunde that I did fe bytwene the South and the
" North gate was an image, as I toke it, of Hercules; for
" he held yn eche hand a ferpent.

" Then I faw the image of a foote-man. *Vibrato gladio*
" *et prætenfo clypeo.*

" Then I faw a braunch with leves folded and wrethin
" into circles.

" Then I faw 2 naked images lying along, the one im-
" bracing the other.

" Then I faw to antique heddes with heere as rofelid yn
" lokkes.

" Then I faw a grey-hound as renning and at the tayle
" of hym was a ftone engravid with great Roman letters,
" but I could pike no fentence out of it.

" Then

" Then I faw another infcription, but the wether had,
" except a few letters, clere defacid.

" Then I faw toward the Weft-gate an image of a man
" embraced with 2 ferpentes. I took it for Laocoon.—

" Betwixt the Wefte and the North-gate.
" I faw two infcriptions of the which fum wordes were
" evident to the reader, the refidue clene defacid.

" Then I faw the image of a naked man.

" Then I faw a ftone having *Cupidines et labrufcas*
" *intercurrentes.*

" Then I faw a table having at eche ende an image vivid
" and florifhed above and benath. In this table was an
" infcription of a tumbe or burial, wher in I faw playnly
" thefe wordes, *viäit annos X X X.* This infcription was
" meately hole but very diffufely written, as letters for hole
" wordes, and 2 or 3 letters conveid in one.

" Then I faw a 2 images, whereof one was of a naked
" manne grafping a ferpent in eche hand, as I took it; and
" this image was not far from the North-gate.

" Such antiquities as were in the waulles from the North-
" gate to the Eft, and from the Eft-gate to the South, hath
                                                  " been

" been defacid by the building of the monaflery, and
" new waulles."

In the year 1522, a fepulchral altar, bearing the following infcription, (in the ufual abbreviations) was dug up
in the village of Walcot.

CAIUS MURRIUS CAII FILIUS ARNIENSIS (TRIBUS)
FORO JULII MODESTUS MILES LEGIONIS SECUND:
: Æ ADJUTRICIS PIÆ FIDELIS JULII SEGUNDI AN:
: NORUM VIGINTI QUINQUE STIPENDIORUM HIC
SITUS EST.

At the fame time this was difcovered;

DIS MANIBUS MARCUS VALERIUS MARCI FILIUS
LATINUS CENTURIO EQUES-MILES LEGIONIS VICE:
: SIMÆ ANNORUM TRIGINTA QUINQUE STIPENDI:
: ORUM VIGINTI IIIC SITUS EST.

Both thefe altars, Camden tells us, were removed by
Mr. Robert Chambers (a great lover of antiquities) who
found them, into his own gardens;¹ and were afterwards
inferted in a wall belonging to the houfe of a Mrs. Chives
near the Crofs Bath, where Horfley faw them about
feventy years ago.

1 Camden Brit. vol. i. p. 91. Edit. 1722.
2 Hors. Brit. Rom. p. 226.

In

In the inner fide of the wall between the North and Weſt gates, were to be feen, in Camden's time, the figure of Hercules holding up his left hand, with his club in the right.—Near it, in a broken piece of ſtone was this inſcription in large and beautiful letters;

> DECURIO COLONIÆ GLEVENSIS VIXIT
> ANNOS OCTOGINTA ET SEX.——

Attached to this, was the repreſentation of leaves folded in, and in a ſepulchral table between two little images, one whereof held an *Amalthean* horn, there were written in charaℭters ſcarcely legible, and badly executed, theſe words;

> DIS MANIBUS SUCCIÆ PETRONIÆ VIXIT ANNOS
> TRES MENSES QUATUOR DIES NOVEM VALERIUS
> PETRONIUS — ET TUICTIA SABINA FILIÆ CARISSIMÆ;
> FECERUNT.[1]

1 Dr. Guidott gives the following account of this ſepulchral altar, together with a different interpretation of its inſcription. " Next to that lower, towards the Weſt-gate is the monument of one of the children of two Romans, *Primulus, Romulus, Vipomulus*, or rather *Viteromulus*, (for that word in the ſtone is ſomewhat difficult to be read) and *Viℭluſarina*, with a longer and exaℭtly Roman inſcription, in a ſepulchral table, between two little images, whereof the one holds the horn of *Amalthæa*, or *cornucopia*; the other bringeth a flying roll or winding liſt, or banner over the left ſhoulder. The inſcription thus—*Diis manibus ſucceſſæ Petroniæ, vixit annos tres, menſes quatuor, dies novem. Veteromulus et Viℭiſarina filiæ Cariſſmæ fecerunt,* Dr. Guidott's Diſcourſe of the Baths. p. 80.

A little

A little below this, on a broken piece of stone, were the
following letters;

V   R   N

I   O   P

Between the West and South gates was a sculpture re-
presenting *Ophiucus* enfolded by a serpent;[1] two masculine
heads with curling locks; a hare running; and a great stone
with these letters:

I   L   I   A

I   L   I   A

A naked man grappling with a soldier; two cumbent
figures embracing each other; a foot-soldier with his
sword and shield; another with his Hasta; and these letters
engraven on a monumental stone;

L I I V S S A

S V X S O

together with the head of Medusa.[2]

---

1 Dr. Wynter is of opinion, that " what Mr. Camden calls something of an
" ancient image of *Hercules* grasping a serpent in his hand, was the local *Hercules*
" with the reed in his hand, his proper ensign, as tutelar deity of waters; and far-
" ther, that his *Ophiucus* enfolded by a serpent between the West and South gate,
" was the figure of the *Greek Æsculapius*, very proper for this place." Treatise of
Bathing, p. 10 and 11. Horsley's Brit. Rom. 329.

2 Camden's Brit. v, i. p. 92.

Dr,

Dr. Guidott mentions a few fragments of Roman mafonry as vifible in his time, which are not now to be found:

" Between the Weft and South-gates were two fierce
" heads, one within the cope of the wall, and another on
" the outfide thereof. Hard by an angry man laying hold
" of a poor peafant, which may be a bold infulting Roman,
" on a diftreffed captivated Briton.

" Two kiffing and clipping each other, which by the
" crook in the right hand of one, and the dog upon the
" other, feem to be a fhepherd and his miftrefs; the dog
" reaching up towards the head of the woman.

" A foot-foldier brandifhing his fword, and bearing out
" his fhield.

" A footman with a truncheon in his right hand.

" A great face, or a giant's head, with hair.

" At Walcot, a parifh adjoining to this city, was found
" a ftone with this infcription:

VIBIA   IVCVNDA

... II . S . E

" Jucunda was an Agnomen of the family of Carvilia, and
" it feems of Vibia, as Lætus of the Claudia and Pomponia."

The

The Doctor mentions the following coins as having been dug up at Bath.—A brafs *Vefpafian*, bearing this legend on the face; IMP. CAES. VESPASIAN. P. F. AVG. *Imperator Cæfar Vefpafianus Pius Felix, Auguftus.* Reverfe: PIETAS AVGVSTI. with the figure of juftice between the letters S. C. *fenatus confultum.*

A filver *Trajan* with this infcription on the face; IMP. TRAIANO. AVG. GER. DAC. P. M. TR. P. *Imperatori Trajano Auguflo Germanico Dacico Pontifici Maximo Tribunitia Poteflate.*---Reverfe; COS. V. P. P. S. P. Q. R. OPTIMO. PRINC. *Confuli quinto Patri Patriæ Senatus Populufque Romanus Optimo Principi.*

A brafs *Caraufius*; the infcription on the face runs thus; IMP. C. CARAVSIVS. P. F. AVG. *Imperator Cæfar Caraufius Pius Felix Auguftus.* On the reverfe, PAX. AVG. *Pax Augufti.*

A brafs *Alexander Severus* with this infcription; IMP. C. M. AVR. SEV. ALEXAND. AVG. *Imperator Cæfar, Marcus Aurelius Severus Alexander Auguftus.* Reverfe; P. M : T. M. R. II COS. P. P. *Pontifex Maximus Tribu nitia Poteflate Secundo Conful Pater Patriæ.*

Mr. Horfley gives an engraving and defcription of a curious ftone he had feen in or near Bath, towards the

clofe of the laft century, which was prefented to Dr. Muf-
grave, and at the time of Horfley's writing, remained in
the poffeffion of his fon.[1]

It reprefents a female head, with the hair highly raifed,
and curioufly dreffed, fuch as appears to have been fafhionable in the time of Juvenal, who ridicules it in the following
lines:

> *Tot premit ordinibus, tot adhuc compagibus altum*
> *Ædificat caput, Andromachen a fronte videbis;*
> *Poft minor, credas aliam.*   Sat : vi. v. 501.

This piece of antiquity is, I believe, at prefent preferved in the ineftimable collection of Lord Pembroke,
at Wilton.

In the repofitory which contains moft of the Remains
of Antiquity treated of in the following fheets, are many
other fragments of Roman Architecture. Thefe confift
of a piece of cornice, elegant in defign, and highly finifhed
in point of execution.—Two fragments of a magnificent
capital of the Corinthian order—parts of a plain column
and pilafter, eighteen inches in diameter. The pediment
of a portal with the figures of Genii fculptured on it, and
feveral *hollow tiles*, twelve inches long, nine deep, and four
broad, with which the ancients formed the flues that heated
their hypocaufts, chambers, paffages, &c.

Guidott p. 76.
[i] Horfley's Brit. Rom. p, 329.

NUMBER

IVLIVS · VITA
LIS FABRICES
IS · LEG · XX · V · V ·
STIPENDIOR
A MIN A XOR XX
IN NATIONE BE
LGA EX · COLEGO
FABRICE ELATV
S · H · S · E ·

No. I

NUMBER I.

━━━━━━━◦◆◦◆◦◆ ✳ ◆◦◆◦◆◦━━━━━━━

JULIUS VITALIS FABRICIESIS LEGIONIS VICESIMÆ
VALERIANÆ VICTRICIS STIPENDIORUM NOVEM
ANNORUM VIGINTI NOVEM NATIONE BELGA EX
COLLEGIO FABRICÆ ELATUS HIC SITUS EST.

NUMBER I. reprefents a monumental ftone, difcovered in the month of October 1708, by certain workmen,
who were digging in, and repairing the road called the
Foffe, originally a Roman way, which now forms the
London road running through Walcot.

It appears to have been erected to the memory of Julius
Vitalis, a native of Belgic Britain, or Weftern England; an
armourer, and ftipendiary of the twentieth legion, who
died at Bath, in the ninth year of his fervice, and the
twenty-ninth of his age.

Many

Many curious particulars are connected with this infcription, which merit individual confideration.

The Cognomen *Vitalis* is not an unufual one; it occurs
frequently in Gruter, and twice in the iufcriptions difcovered in this country. **Dr.** Gale has preferved one, wherein
mention is made of *Quintus Virius Vitalis*;[1] and Horfley
gives us another, found at Drawdikes, in Cumberland,
which commemorates a foldier of the fame name with the
one defcribed in this monumental ftone.[2] It cannot, however, be fuppofed to refer to the fame perfon; fince the
former was a Centurion in a Prætorian cohort, and the latter
only a common ftipendiary, of no dignity or command.

The word *Fabriciefis* (for Fabricienfis) denotes the employment of the deceafed; and informs us that he had
been a member of the *College* of *Armourers*—What the
bufinefs of this fociety, and the laws by which it was
regulated, were, we learn from certain articles in the
Theodofian and Juftinian codes.—It there appears, that in
the later periods of the Roman empire, the army fmiths
were erected into a formal company, under the controul
and management of an officer denominated *Primicerius*.[3]—
That the employment of this body, was to make arms for
the ufe of the foldiery, at public forges or fhops, called

1 Gale Anton. Itin : p. 2. 0.
2 COHORTIS QUARTÆ PRÆTORIANÆ POSUIT CENTURIA JULII VITALIS.
Hors: Cumberland xxxviii.
4 Panciroilus Not: Col : 1498.

Fabricæ,

Fabricæ, erected in their camps, cities, towns, and military ſtations.—That theſe arms, when forged, were to be delivered to an officer appointed to receive them, who laid them up in the arſenals for public ſervice.—That to prevent any abuſe in this important branch of military œconomy, and to enſure its proper and methodical management, no perſon was permitted to forge arms for the imperial ſervice unleſs he were previouſly admitted a member of the ſociety of the *Fabri.*—That to ſecure the continuance of their labours after they had been inſtructed in the art, a certain yearly ſtipend was ſettled on each *Faber*; who, (as well as his children) was prohibited from leaving the employ, till he had attained the office of *Primicerius.*—And finally, that no one might quit his buſineſs without detection, a mark or ſtigma was impreſſed on the arm of each, as ſoon as he became a member of the college.[1]

That a club or company of this trade was ſettled, and a public *Fabrica* eſtabliſhed at Bath, during the reſidence of the Romans there, may be fairly inferred, both from the conſideration and importance of the place in thoſe times, and the expreſſion, in our inſcription, *ex Collegio Fabricæ elatus*; which denotes that the Fabrica was in a *neighbouring city.* For it hath been obſerved by the learned Selden, that the terms *efferre* and *deducere,* in monumental inſcriptions, are applicable only to thoſe funerals, in which the bodies were brought from an *immediately adjoining city,*

[1] Cod. Theod: lib. x. Tit: 22. Cod. Juſt: ix. Novel: Theod: xliii.

town, or ſtation, and interred in its contiguous and appio-, priate public burying ground.

The deceaſed is further deſcribed as belonging to the 20th legion; the titles of which, though contrary to general practice, I have given *Valerian* and Victorious. My interpretation is countenanced by the authority of Dion, who exprefsly ſays, "that the 20th legion ſtationed in Britain, in his time, was called Valerian and Victorious."[1] There were, it is true, more 20th legions than one; but that which received its name from ſome commander called *Valerius*, is the only one which appears from hiſtorical records, or inſcriptions, to have ſerved in Britain.[1] This body of troops came over in the reign of Claudius, and continued here nearly as long as the Romans retained poſſeſſion of the country.—*Deva* or Cheſter was their head quarters for the better part of three centuries; but our inſcription leads us to conclude, they might have changed that ſtation for Bath, previous to their departure

---

1 Οι εικοροι οι κ̣, Ουαλεριειοι και νικητορες ωνομασμενοι, και οι Βρ̣ιταννια τη αιω οντις, εςιναι αιτες, εμοι δοκειν, &c. Lib. LV. P 564.

1 The Roman legions took their Cognomens from various circumſtances. Some-times from the names of the *Emperors* who formed them; ſuch as Legio Auguſta: Claudiana; Galbiana; Flavia; Trajana; Antoniana.—Sometimes from the *provinces* they had conquered; ſuch as Parthica; Scythica; Gallica; Arabica; Hiſpanienſis; or from the *place* in which they were firſt ſtationed, after being embodied, ſuch as Italica; Forenſis; Cyreniaca;—or from the *names* of the *deities* to whom the Emper-ors that formed them were more particularly attached, ſuch as Minerva; Apollinaris —orlaſtly from certain particular *circumſtances* by which they were diſtinguiſhed, ſuch as Legio Germina; Adjutrix; Martia; Victrix: Ferrata; Fulminatrix; Alauda; Rapax; Primigenia: and ſo forth.—Vide Dempſter Antiq. Rom. c. 4. p.,966.

from

from England. The shape of the letters, and the ligatures and complications which appear in the fifth and seventh lines, mark the infcription for a late one; and authorize us to fuppofe, the monument might be erected towards the clofe of the fourth century, about which time, it is probable the 20th legion left this kingdom.

The 4th and 5th lines contain a notification of the age of the deceafed, and his time of fervice; by which we find he had entered rather later than was common into military employ.—The age at which the Roman youth affumed the *toga militaris*, or foldier's habit, was feventeen;[1] a practice beautifully alluded to in the following lines of Silius Italicus.

> *Pubefcit caftris miles, Galeaque teruntur*
> *Nondum fignatæ flavâ lanug'ne malæ.*[1]

But although the *enrollment* of the youth took place at the age of feventeen, it is manifeft both from the above infcription and many others in Gruter's collection, that they were not always called immediately into actual fervice.--- The legions being previoufly compleat, or many other circumftances, might occafion a confiderable interval to elapfe from the time of nomination, to their being incorporated; and as, during this period, they were not intitled to a

---

1 Liv: 3. Decad. Lib. 5.
2 Sil: Ital: Lib, 2.

ftipendium,

ſtipendium, or pay, they were of courſe not confidered as
legionaries, though they had aſſumed the military garb.---
Horſley has preſerved another curious infcription, dug up
about two hundred years ago, in the then village of Walcot, commemorating a Centurion of the fame twentieth
legion, who appears to have been an exception to the
general practice of not commencing the military career
till after the age of ſeventeen, fince at his deceaſe, at
thirty-five, he had ſerved twenty campaigns, and confequently muſt have been in actual employ when only fifteen
years old.

The words *Natione Belga* (for *Belgica*), inform us that
the deceaſed was a Briton, probably a native of Somerſet-
ſhire, which county conſtituted a part of the diviſion called
by the Romans *Britannia Belgica*.

This ſtone is at preſent fixed in the wall at the eaſtern
end of the Abbey-church; is ſeven feet four inches in
height, and thirty-four inches in breadth.

ɪ Dɪs Mᴀɴɪʙus Mᴀʀcus Vᴀʟᴇʀɪus Mᴀʙɢɪ ғɪʟɪus Lᴀᴛɪɴus cᴇɴᴛuʀɪo
ɪꜰQuᴇs ᴍɪʟᴇs Lᴇɢɪoɴɪs ᴠɪcᴇsɪᴍᴀ ᴀɴɴoʀuᴍ ᴛʀɪɢɪɴᴛᴀ QuɪɴQuᴇ sᴛɪᴘᴇɴ-
ᴠɪoʀuᴍ ᴠɪɢɪɴᴛɪ ᴍɪc sɪᴛus ᴇsᴛ. Horſley Brit; Rom; Somerſet: No. ɪɪɪ;

NUMBER

No. II.

NUMBER II.

LUCIUS VITELLIUS MANTANI FILIUS TANCINUS CIVIS
HISPANIÆ CAURIESIS EQUITUM ALÆ VETTONUM
CENTURIO ANNORUM XXXXVI. STIPENDIORUM
XXVI. HIC SITUS EST.

THE inferior part of this monumental ſtone, containing
the above inſcription, was erected to the memory of
Lucius Vitellius Tancinus, the ſon of *Mantanus,* a citizen of
Caurium, in Spain, centurion of the Vettonenſian auxiliary
horſe;[1] who died in the forty-ſixth year of his age, and the
twenty-

---

[1] " Altera pars exercitûs auxilia erant. Sic autem dicebantur ii milites qui a ſociis,
" vel e fœderatis gentibus mittebantur." Dempſter p. 964. The Roman auxiliaries
were the troops levied in thoſe cities and towns, on whoſe inhabitants the title and
privileges of Roman citizens had been conferred. Theſe were formed into cohorts,
and attached to particular legions, of which they made a part, and were denominated
auxiliaries. When the army was marſhalled for battle, they were uſually placed at
the two extremities of the line. Hence the auxiliary foot were often termed *Cornua*
or horns; and the horſe, *Alæ* or wings. " Alæ dictæ ſunt exercitus, Equitum ordinis,
" quod circum legiones, dextra ſiniſtraque tanquam Alæ in avium corpore locoban-
" tur." Dempſter, p. 989. The politic wiſdom of the Romans induced them to
continue

twenty-fixth of his military fervice. This, and the fragment now placed above, and attached to it, have been hitherto confidered as conflituting one piece of fculpture; but the erroneoufnefs of the opinion will be fufficiently obvious, when the refpective dimenfions of the two ftones, and the proportions of their figures are attended to, which prove that the parts had no connection originally with each other.—Add to this alfo, they were found in places widely feparate; the upper part near to Grofvenor Gardens, and the lower one on the feite of the prefent Market-houfe.

The former has been conjectured, and with fome probability, to be the moiety of a monumental ftone erected to the honor of *Geta*, one of the fons of *Septimius Severus*, who, about the year of our Lord one hundred and ninety-fix, was left by his father in this part of the kingdom to adminifter juftice, during his abfence on a Northern expedition.

One prominent feature in the character of this prince was an unbounded paffion for horfes; a foible which the degenerate fenate of the times took care to flatter, by

continue to the auxiliaries the ufe of fuch arms, as they had been in the habit of handling in their own countries, and in the management of which they had of courfe attained to great excellence and expertnefs. And hence it was, that their armies were provided with the beft warriors of every kind, that the world could produce. The Balearic iflands, Minorca and Majorca furnifhed them with flingers —Crete with bowmen—Numidia with light horfe—Spain with heavy cavalry— Greece with engineers—and Rhodes and Epirus gave confequence to their marine, by fending admirable fhip-wrights, and experienced naval commanders.

impreffing

impreffing on his coins, the figure of the youth in the character of *Caftor*,¹ cloathed in a military equeftrian drefs.²—And as this was confidered on the continent as an high compliment, it is not unlikely that fycophants would be found in the province where he commanded, to pay him fimilar adulation; and to gratify his vanity, by erecting altars, exhibiting him in his favorite character.

The upper fculpture is much defaced; but fufficient of it remains to fhew that it is an equeftrian figure, bearing in his left hand a *parma*,³ and in his right a *hafta pura*;⁴ and purfuing a flying enemy. The under one, reprefented a Spanifh, horfeman in the garb of his natioh, riding over a proftrate foe.

The name *Tancinus* feems to have been a Spanifh cognomen, fince it occurs in an infcription found in the province of Lufitania, and preferved in Gruter's collection; " *M: Licinius Tancinus*—II : S: E :"⁵

The deceafed foldier is alfo mentioned to have been a citizen of *Caurium*,⁶ a town of Lufitania, in the diftrict of Eftrema-

1 Caftor gaudet equis, ovo prognatus eodem
Pugnis. Hor.
2 Oiefelius Thes. Sed Num. in Verb. *Geta*.
3 A fmall light, commodious fhield or target, adapted by its fize, for the cavalry. Brevis clypeus, rotundus et undique par. Not: in Æn: 10. v. 800.
4 A miffile weapon or fpear, with which the horfe were furnifhed, having for the fake of lightnefs, no iron about it.—Pura Juvenis qui mittitur hafta. Æn: lib. 6. 6.
5 Grut: Infcrip: 917—8.
6 The word is written *Cauriefis* for *Caurienfis*; the letter N being dropped—This omiffion is not unufual in ancient infcriptions, of which there are many extant,

wherein

Eſtremadura,¹ inveſted with municipal privileges; that is, enjoying the uſe of its own ancient laws and conſtitutions, together with the rights and franchiſes of Roman citizens.² The *Vettones* were a neighbouring people, who furniſhed excellent heavy-armed horſe levies to their Roman maſters. Its *ala*, or wing, here ſpoken of, was probably attached to the twentieth legion; in this *Tancinus* bore the office of centurion; a command ſomewhat analogous to the captaincy of a troop in our ſervice.

Points or ſtops in ancient inſcriptions are good criteria of their antiquity. In the earlier periods of the empire, theſe conſiſted merely of ſimple round dots. About the time of Antoninus Pius, however, the workmen began to deviate from this ſimplicity; and becoming gradually more capricious, introduced at length ſtops of various forms;

wherein the engraver ſeems to have ſpelled the word according to the popular mode of pronunciation, which frequently neglected to found the *N* before the letter *S*, when it occurred in the middle of a word. Phil. Trans. No. 357. Alſo laſt inſcription in verb : *Fabricieſis* pro *Fabricienſis*—This practice was gradually admitted into the Roman orthography ; and being countenanced by Auguſtus Cæſar (as we learn from Suetonius) it ſoon gained ſuch a footing as to be adopted into the language of the beſt ſcholars·—" Orthographiam, id eſt formulam rationemque ſcri" bendi, a Grammaticis inſtitutam, non adeo cuſtodiit ; ac videtur eorum potius " ſequi opinionem, qui perinde ſcribendum, ac loquamur, exiſtiment. Nam quod " ſæpe non literas modo, ſed ſyllabas aut permutat, aut præterit, communis homi" num error eſt." Sueton: in Vit: Aug: c. 88.

1 Luſitaniæ opp. Ptol : quæ et Caura vulgo Coria. In Eſtremadura Region : juxta Alagonem Flav; qui ſeptem inde Leuc : cadit in Tagum ; 5 Leuc : a confinio Portugalliæ, &c. Hoffmanni Lexicon, Tom. i. P. 778.

2 Municipium oppidum erat jure civium Romanorum donatum. Roſinus Ant : Rom ; Lib : x, c. xxii.

angular,

angular, triangular, leaf-fhaped, and rhomboidal. The form of thofe in our infcription are of this fantaftical nature, and prove it to be a very late one; probably coeval with that which we laft confidered.

The initials II : S : E : which merely notify that the deceafed was interred near to the ftone that commemorates him, conveys a pleafing idea of the fimplicity of the Romans with refpect to their monumental infcriptions.— Thefe wife people were aware, that as " the floried urn, the " animated buft," or the tinfel of fepulchral flattery, could not give future renown to departed infamy, fo neither were they aids, to which worth and virtue had occafion to look, for the praife of pofterity ;

" The *actions* of the *juft*
" Smell fweet, and bloffom in the duft."

This monumental ftone is alfo fixed in the wall at the Eaftern end of the Abbey-church—its height is five-feet ; the breadth of the lower part is 36 inches ; of the upper part 28 inches.

DEAE
SVLIM
NERVAE
SVLINVS
MATV
RIFIL
VSLM

No. III.

NUMBER III.

DEÆ SULINI MINERVÆ SULINUS MATURI FILIUS VOTUM
SOLVIT LIBENS MERITO.

THIS is a votive altar, turned up in 1774, as the work-men were removing the rubbiſh from the head of the ſpring of the Hot Bath. It appears to have been ſolemnly dedi-cated to the tutelary deity of the Bath waters; (to whom the devotee has given the loçal title of *Sulinis*) and was probably intended as a grateful return for benefit received from the uſe of theſe ſprings, which were under her im-mediate protection and patronage.

On confidering the character of the extraordinary people, by one of whom this memorial of pious ſuper-ſtition was erected, we cannot help remarking a very ſtriking feature of it; the warm ſpirit of religion by which it was diſtinguiſhed from the earlieſt period of the com-monwealth, to the loweſt times of the empire. Originally incorporated with their conſtitution by the great Roman
legiſlator

legiflator Numa, (who knew full well that religion was absolutely neceffary to the eftablifhment and fecurity of civil government) the principle gradually expanded, as the Republic increafed; entered into all their public concerns, and domeftic tranfactions; entwined itfelf with every profeffion in which they engaged, and was connected with every plan which they undertook.—It is to this religioufnefs of fpirit, that we are to attribute the numerous temples, altars, and other memorials of their devotion, which we meet with fo abundantly in every place where the Romans had been for any confiderable time ftationary. If an evil were to be deprecated, or a bleffing invoked, the votary entered into a folemn engagement to raife fome monument of his gratitude to the benign being who fhould hear his prayer, and comply with his petition; a vow which fuccefs never rendered him unmindful to perform.[1] As the falutary waters of Bath were generally reforted to by the Romans for nearly four centuries, it is probable that a very large number of thefe

---

[1] Votum folvit libens merito.—He *willingly* fulfilled the vow which he had defervedly made, was the language in which the Roman expreffed his readinefs to obferve this facred engagement.—All the ancients indeed were very ftrict in this re pect.—It is a precept of Pythagoras ;

Αβανατους μιν πρωτα Θιυς, νομω ως διακειται,

Τιμα, και σιβε ορκον.—that is, an oath or vow made to them.

And Æneas before he attends to other preffing concerns, takes care to fulfill his vows to the Gods.

Æneas (quanquam et fociis dare tempus humandis
Præcipitant curæ, turbataque funere mens eft)
Vota Deum primo Victor folvebat Eoö.—

Virg: En: 11—2.

votive

votive altars would be erected to the tutelary deity of their springs, by thofe who left them with renovated health and vigour; and, doubtlefs, the foundations of the prefent city cover many precious remains of this nature, which, if difcovered, would afford further examples of the united art and piety of the conquerors of the world.

With refpect to the *fituation* of thefe altars, no particular rule feems to have been obferved. They were many times placed in the temples of the divinity to whom they were dedicated ; and as often erected near the public ways, or other frequented fpots, that they might be confpicuous teftimonies of the kindnefs of the propitious deity, and the pious gratitude of his worfhipper. The dimunitive fize of the altar under confideration, and its being found on the fcite of the ancient temple of Minerva, render it probable, that it was originally placed within the walls of that magnificent fane.

It was a principle of policy with the Romans to adopt into their own mythology, the various deities of the different nations they fubdued; a practice that difplayed the profoundeft knowledge of the human mind.[1] For as there is nothing that fpeaks more powerfully to the hopes and fears of man than religion: fo there is nothing which makes a deeper impreffion on the foul, that is retained with

---

[1] It is a remark of Dionyfius Halicareffenfis, that there were fix hundred different kinds of religions, or facred rites exercifed at Rome. Jortin's Remarks on Eccl.: Hift; v. i. p. 371.

C

greater

greater tenacity, or renounced with more reluctance.
It was this indulgence shewn to the religious prejudices of
the conquered nations; this allowance of the free exer-
cise of their accustomed modes of worship, that both
facilitated the Roman successes, and gave them stability;
that stripped conquest of half its horrors, and made the
yoke of servitude tolerably easy. With respect to Britain,
indeed, it was necessary for them to depart, in some degree,
from their usual moderation; for such was the wonderful
influence which the Druids had obtained over the minds
of their disciples, that all the arts of Roman policy would
have been insufficient to reduce the Britons to order and
subordination, had they permitted a superstition so ferocious
and indomitable to have continued.—To modify it in any
shape, or to incorporate it with their own system, was
impossible; since the profound veneration and implicit
deference paid by the conquered nation to the ministers of
their religion, as well as the savage nature of it,[1] effectually
precluded all hope of reconciling them to a milder system,
whilst Druidism existed. Prudence therefore dictated to
the Romans to forego, on this occasion, their general
lenity; and this wonderful superstition (with all its bloody
rites), was at length consumed in the flames of the sacred
groves of Mona.[2]

It

---

1 Cæsar de Bell: Gall: Lib: vi.

Et vos barbaricos ritus, moremque sinistrum.

Sacrorum Druidæ positis repetistis ab armis—Lucan Phar: L.: i. 445.

2 The dreadful ferocity with which Druidism inspired even the weaker sex,
is well described by Tacitus; a ferocity, that, for a time, disturbed the steady
bravery of the Roman legions. " Stabat pro litore diversa acies, densa armis vi-

" risq

It is to be obferved, however, that this harfhnefs of the Romans was confined, in a great degree, to the more Northern, and North-Weftern parts of Britain. — The communication which the Southern or Belgic principalities had for fome time preferved, through the medium of commerce, with the inhabitants of the continent, had improved their manners, and foften:d the favage character of their ancient fuperftition. They had difcarded the fanguinary practices of Druidifm, and imbibed fo much of the fpirit of Polytheifm, as to admit the exiftence of all thofe fubordinate intelligences, with which the orthodox Pagan, believed every part of created fpace to be filled.—By them, therefore, the mythology of their conquerors would be readily received; and the divinities of South-Britain were quickly affociated with the deities of Rome.

The Goddefs SULINIS, mentioned in our infcription, feems to have been a local deity of this kind.—The altars, No. 5 and 6, are dedicated to her individually, with no additional name; and as they appear to be the grateful offerings

" rifque, intercurfantibus feminis; in modum Furiarum, vefte ferali, crinibus
" dejectis, faces præferebant. Druidæ circum preces diras fublatis ad cælum mani-
" bus fundentes, novitate afpectus perculere milites, ut quafi hærentibus membris,
" immobile corpus vulneribus præberent. Dein cohortationibus ducis, et fe ipfi
" ftimulantes, ne muliebre et fanaticum agmen pavefcerent, inferunt figna, fternuntque
" obvios, et igni fuo involvunt. Præfidium pofthac impofitum victis, excifique luci
" fævis fuperftitionibus facri nam eruore captivo adelere aras, et hominum fibris
" confulere Deos fat habebant. Tacit: Ann: Lib: xiv. 30,

of

of certain invalids who had received benefit by the use of
the waters, it is reasonable to suppose she was the tutelary
deity, or Nymph of the Bath springs. To these imaginary
beings it was very usual with the ancients to erect altars,
and make vows.—Indeed the worship of rivers and springs,
was one of the most early superstitions that misled man-
kind. The limpid element being considered as an admirable
emblem of the purity of the great first cause, it was soon
made one of the intermediate vehicles of communication
with the deity. This practice insensibly begot the idea of
there being an inherent sanctity in the element itself; an
opinion, to which ignorance and error gradually added the
more absurd one, of inferior Deities inhabiting, or pre-
siding over each fountain, spring, and river.

In process of time the superstition became almost universal; and there was scarcely a country which did not
pay divine honors to its own streams.[1]

Egypt, famed for mental error and moral darkness, first
adopted the practice, and regarded with peculiar veneration, the river Nile, the father of their country, the great
source of their wealth and plenty.[2] From hence, this
superstition flowed, with many others, into Greece; and
as early as Homer's time vows were made, and religious
rites offered to rivers. To the Thessalian stream Sperchius,

[1] Επι τ8 και ποταμων τιμη. Max. Tyrius. C. 8. P. 79.
[2] Νιλοι τον πατιρα και σωτηρα της γης. Plutarch, Symp. L. 8 P. 729.

(that

(that is to the genius or deity fuppofed to refide in it), Peleus, the father of Achilles, promifed to facrifice an Hecatomb; fifty fheep, and the flowing locks of his fon, if he returned fafely to his native land.

Σπερχει, αλλως σοι γε πατηρ ηρησατο Πηλευς,
Κεισε με νοςησαντα φιλην ες παιριδα γαιαν,
Σοι δε κομην κερεαν, ρεξειν θ'ιερην εκατομβην·
Πεντεκοντα δ'ενορχα παρ αυτόθι μηλ' ιερευσιν
Ες πηγας, οθι τοι τεμεν Θ βωμος τε θυης.[1]

The Romans receiving the fanciful mythology of Greece, adopted, of courfe, this branch of it. They confecrated particular days to the worfhip of the fubordinate intelligences who prefided over the fprings and rivers of their country; on which, amongft other tokens of veneration, fhewn to them, chaplets of flowers were caft into the

---

[1] Sperchie, fruftrà tibi utique pater vovit Peleus,
Illuc me reverfum dilectum in patriam terram,
Tibiquecomam abfciffurum, mactaturumque facram Hecatomben :
Quinquaginta infuper mafculas ibidem oves facrificaturum
Ad fontes, ubi tibi ager facer altaréque odoratum.

ΙΛΙΑΔ. Ψ. 144. The facrifice of the *head of hair* to Rivers, was ufual with the an. cients, as the Scholiaft obferves; who alfo gives us the Reafon for it. Εθος ην τοις αρχαιοις μετα το παρακμασαι της ηλικιας, τας κομας; αποκιρειν τοις ποταμοις· τουτης γας ενεμιζον των αναιρεφων αιτιας εναι. Schol: in Loc.

Virgil makes his hero Æneas, on his reaching the mouth of the Tyber, immediately invoke the nymphs and unknown deities of the ftream,

Nymphafque et adhuc ignota precatur
Numina :—

Virg. Æne: vii. L. 137.

ftreams,

ſtreams, and crowns of the ſame were placed on the borders of the wells.[1]

But this ſuperſtition far from being confined to Egypt, Greece, and Rome, infeſted, as I have before hinted, moſt other nations. Perſians,[2] Parthians,[3] and Phrygians,[4] bowed before the tutelary gods of their rivers; and the numerous Celtic tribes worſhiped the Genii or Dæmons, who peopled the various ſtreams that flowed through their extenſive country.[5]

From theſe circumſtances, it appears to be more than probable, that the Goddeſs SULINIS was the inferior intelligence, to whom the Britons attributed the tutelage of the Bath ſprings; and to whom they gave the Cognomen

1 Varro Lib: 5. de Ling. Lat.
2 Σέουνται ποταμυς μάλιςα, Herod. I. 1. c. 138.
3 Parthis. præcipua omnibus veneratio. Jnſtin L. 4: c. 3.
4 Φρυγες οι περι Κελαινας ημρμενοι τιμωσι ποταμυς δυο, Μαρσυραν και Μαιανδραν. Στωσι φρυγες τοις ποταμοις. Max. Tyr. Diſſ. 8. P. 87.
5 Thulitæ complures Genios colunt. Aereos, terreſtres, marinos, et alia minora Dæmonia, quæ in aquis fontium et fluminum verſari dicuntur. Procopius Goth: Lib: 2. The Germanic nations alſo, which bordered on Italy, held ſimilar opinions; as is manifeſt from a paſſage in Tacitus; where, in anſwer to a propoſal made in the ſenate, for altering the courſe of the Tyber, an objection was made that the intended alteration might interfere with the religion of the Roman allies, who had dedicated groves and altars to their national ſtreams. Spectandas etiam religiones ſociorum, qui ſacra, et lucos, et aras patriis amnibus dicaverint. Tacit: Annal. Lib: i. c. 79. p. 46. Edit: Elziv.

MINERVA

MINERVA, becaufe in her attributes and attachments fhe
bore fome refemblance to that Deity.

This altar is about thirty inches in height, and twelve in
width.[1]

---

1 This altar is placed, at prefent, on the great ftaircafe of the Guild-hall, and
with it, is another of nearly fimilar fhape and fize.—The infcription of the altar is
fo defaced, that I could not make it out; in the Hiftory of Somerfetfhire it ftands
as follows : (vol, i. p. 14).

DEAE DIA
NAE SACRATI
SSIMAE VOTV
M SOLVIT V
VETTIVS BE
NIGNVS. L. M.

D   M
CCALPVRNVS
ECEPTVS SAC
DOS DEAE SV
LS VIXA LXXV
CAPV'N ATRIFC
SA PTC°NVX
F   C

No. IV.

NUMBER IV.

DIIS MANIBUS. CAIUS CALPURNIUS RECEPTUS SACER-
DOS DEÆ SULINIS VIXIT ANN LXXV. — — —
CALPURNIA CONJUNX FACIENDUM CURAVIT.

THE àltar we are now to illuſtrate is a ſepulchral
Cippus, commemorating *Caius Calpurnius*, a prieſt of the
Goddeſs *Sulinis*, who died at the age of ſeventy-five. His
wife *Calpurnia* cauſed this tribute to his memory to be erected. It was dug up by ſome labourers about two years
ſince, as they were working in Sydney-Gardens.

The ancients, both Greeks and Romans, held every
thing which regarded the dead, in great veneration; and
the laws relative to ſepulture, funeral obſequies, &c. make
no ſmall part of their legal inſtitutions.

Previous to the publication of the twelve tables, it was
cuſtomary with the latter, to burn, or inter the bodies
H   of

of the departed, within the walls of the city.[1] But as fe-
several inconveniencies were experienced from the practice,
one article of this code was exprefsly levelled againſt it ;
Hominem mortuum, in urbe, ne sepelito, neve, urito;[2] a law
which did not regard Rome alone, but extended itſelf to
every city of the empire.

This prohibition obliged the Romans to ſeek out other
places of interment; and it was not long before they
adopted the cuſtom of burying the dead, and performing
the obſequies, a little without their towns, erecting the
ſepulchres, by the ſide of the public high-ways.—A practice to which they were led by the two-fold reaſon of thus
rendering their piety and gratitude more conſpicuous ; and
exciting the numerous travellers and paſſengers to ſerious
reflection on the precariouſneſs of life, and the certainty o
diſſolution;[3]

That theſe public roads were the general places of ſepulture, is evident both from the numerous funeral altars
diſcovered immediately contiguous to them, and from
various alluſions to the practice in the works of the poets.

---

1 In their own gardens, or near their own reſidences were frequently the placeſ
of interment.

   Sedibus hunc refer ante ſuis, et conde ſepulchro. Æn : L: 5.

2 Cicero Lib. 2. de Leg. Credo (inquit Cicero) vel propter ignis Periculum.

3 Monumenta enim in ſepulchris ſecundum viam ſunt, quæ prætereuntes admo-
neant et ſe fuiſſe, et illos eſſe mortales. Varro, Lib: 5. de Ling : Lat.

Thus

Thus Juvenal——
>——*Experiar quid concedatur in illos,*
>*Quorum Flaminiá tegitur Cinis, atque Latiná.*[1]

Alſo Propertius——
>*Dii faciant mea ne terrá locet oſſa frequenti*
>*Qua facit aſſiduo tramite vulgus iter.*[2]

Again——
>*Non juvat in media nomen habere viá——*[3]

And laſtly——
>*Si te forté meo ducet via proxima buſto.*[4]

But that the ſepulchral altars thus erected in public and expoſed ſituations, might be protected from deſtruction, or violation, the Roman law made them a particular object of its cognizance.[5]

It was an inſtitution originially of *Solon*, afterwards adopted by the *Decemviri*, who digeſted the twelve tables, that the perſon who defaced a ſepulchre; broke it; eraſed its inſcription; or beat down the monument, ſhould ſuffer

1 Juv : Sat. 1. in. fin.
2 Lib: 3. Eleg: 16.
3 Id.
4 Id. Lib. 2. l. 85.
5 Sepulchorum autem ſanctitas in ipſo ſolo eſt quod nullo vi moveri, neque deleri poteſt. Dempſter's Antiq: Rom : p. 784.

death,

death.' Nay, fo careful were the laws, of thefe man-
fions of the dead, that even a near approach to them was
exprefsly forbidden, except at the time of performing the
obfequies, or offering the annual facrifices.²

Perhaps, however, all thefe legal reftraints would have
been infufficient to guard them from wanton violence, had
they not been defended alfo by the fanction of fuperftition.
It was this powerful principle that operated moft ftrongly
in their favour ; and rendered them objects of awful veneration, even with the loweft populace, who avoided, with
the moft careful circumfpection, every fpot where the
afhes of the dead were depofited.—The pious Polytheifts
were firmly perfuaded that the violation of them was a
fin of no lefs magnitude than facrilege ; a crime which
would inevitably draw down upon the guilty wretch, the
exemplary vengeance of Heaven ;—

H γαρ οδε ςαλαν Αφαρνϊη εξανεχθταν
Τυμβω αναρρηξας ταχεως Μεσανιϴ Ιδας,
Μελλε καϑιγννϑοιο Βαλων σφειεροιο Φουηx.
Αλλα Ζευς ϛταμυνε χεραν δε οι εκβαλε τυκϑαν,
Μαρμαρον, αυϑον δε Φλογεω συνεϕλεξε κεραυνω.³

1 Cic : de Leg : Lib : 2.
2 Plutarchus in Vit : Solon.
   3 Nam profecto columnam in Apharei extantem
      Sepulchro erutam celeriter Meffenius Idas
      Projecturus erat in fratris fui interfectorem :
      Sed Iupiter opem tulit, manibufq illius excuffit fabrefactum
      Marmor, ipfumq flammeo combuffit fulmine.
      Theoc : Id : H. C. 207.

The

The initials D. M. at the head of the infcription inform us, that the altar was dedicated to the *Dii Manes*.

With refpect to thefe imaginary beings, the ancients do not appear to have had any precife or determinate ideas.[1] — Sometimes they were taken for the infernal deities ; and in this fenfe they feem to be invoked in the fourth Georgic ;

Quo fletu Manes, quâ Numina voce moveret.[2]

Sometimes for the fhade or ghoft of the deceafed, as appears to be the meaning of the expreffion in the following paffage ;

Libabat cine Andromache, manesque vocabat
Hectoreum ad tumulum.[3]

For it is to be remarked, the ancients were of opinion, that at the diffolution of any perfon, his *anima*, foul, or fpiritual part, was wafted into Heaven ; his body remained in the earth where it had been depofited ; and his *Umbra, Imago, Shade,* or *Ghoft,* defcended to the infernal regions.

1 Sumuntur pro mortuorum animis, et pro loco ipfo inferorum, ubi animi degunt, et pro diis ipfis inferorum.—Vide Not : in Virg : Georg : Lib. iv. L. 469. Animas Hominum Dæmones effe, et ex hominibus fieri *Lares,* fi meriti boni fint : *Lemures* five *Larvas,* fi mali ; *Manes* autem cum incertum eft bonorum eos, five malorum effe meritorum—Plotinus apud, Aug. civit : p. Dei. 81. ix, 11.

2 Virg : Georg : iv. L. 505.

3 Æn : Lib : iii. v. 302,

But

But whatever their notions might be in refpect to the *Manes* themfelves, yet they appear to have regarded them with the moft fcrupulous fuperftition.—The *Cippi*, as I have before obferved, were efteemed facred. Particular facrifices were appointed to be offered upon them ; and certain anniverfary days fet apart for celebrating thefe holy rites.[1]

On the ninth, and thirtieth days after interment, the relations of the deceafed vifited the tomb, and paid a variety of honors to the manes of the departed.—Honey, wine, water, milk, and barley-flour, were poured, and fprinkled upon the altar;

Χοας χεομεν πασι νεκυεσσιν.
Πρωτα μελικρητω, μετεπειτα δε ηδεϊ οινω,
Το τριτον αυθ' υδατι επι δ' αλφιτα λευκα παλυνον:

1 Thefe days were called *Feralia*, and occurred about the middle of February, Ovid in his Fafti has enumerated the rites, then obferved :

   Eft honor et tumulis animas placare paternas,
     Parvaque in extructas munera ferre Pyras.
   Parva petunt manes, pietas pro Divite grata eft
     Munere, non avidos Styx habet ima deos.
   Tegula porrectis fatis eft velata coronis,
     Et fparfæ fruges parvaque mica falis.
   Inque mero mollita Ceres, violæque folutæ :
     Hæc habeat media tefta relicta via.
   Nec majora veto, fed et his placabitis umbra eft :
     Adde preces pofitis et fua verba focis.

2 Hom : Odyff; b. v. 36.

Sometimes

Sometimes a libation of blood was made; with which
the ancients fuppofed the Manes, or Ghofts, were much
delighted.

Inferimus tepido fpumantia cymbia laЭe,—
*Sanguinis et facri pateras.*¹

And again, at the anniverfary of Anchifes' death, facred
blood is mingled with the other libations.

Hic duo viti mero libens carchefia Baccho,
*Fundit humi, duo laЭe novo, fanguine facro.*²

Certain flowers, alfo, which were efteemed to be particularly agreeable to the infernal deities, were on thefe occafions, laid on the tomb, or fcattered around it ;

*Purpureofque jacit flores, ac talia fatur.*³

And the monument itfelf, was folemnly anointed with
precious unguents and fweet perfumes;

Afferet huc unguenta mihi fertifque fepulchrum
*Ornabit, Cuftos ad mea bufta fedens.*⁴

1 Æn : Lib : iii. vr 56.
2 Æn : Lib : v. v. 77.
3 Id; Lib. v. v. 79.
4 Propert : Eleg : Lib : 33 Eleg : 15.

An

An attention which Anacreon, in the true fpirit of jollity, intreats, may be paid to himfelf whilft living, rather than to his tomb-ftone, when he is no more ;

τι σε δει λιθον μυριζειν
Τι δε γη χεειν ματαια;
εμε μαλλον, ως ετι ζω,
μυρισον; ροδοις δε κρατα
πυκαζον.[1]

As the fepulchral altar we are confidering has no *focus*, it appears to be one of thofe which they termed αναιμακτοι και εμπυροι, not intended for fire or blood, but merely for the oblation of prayers, and the occafional offering of funeral flowers, &c.

Manibus date lilia plenis :
Purpureos fpargam flores, Animamque nepotis
Hic faltem accumulem donis, et fungar inani
Munere;[2]

The *Calpurnian* family, to which the deceafed belonged, was one of the nobleft in Rome. According to Plutarch, it traced its origin from Calpo, the fon of Numa Pompilius; an affertion which Ovid corroborates;

1 Anacreon Od. δ; Quid te opus eft Lapidem meum inungere ?
Quid autem terræ infundere vana ?
Me magis, ut adhuc vivo,
Unge, rofis autem caput meum
Necte,

2 Æn : vi. v. 883.

Nam

(33)

Nam quid memorare necesse est,
Ut Domus a Calpo nomen Calpurnia ducat?

A perfon of the fame family name, with the Cognomen
Agricola, was proprætor in Britain, under Marcus Aurelius;[1] and Quintus Calpurnius Concellinus was Legate
here under Caracalla. Whether either of thefe commanders were connected with the Prieft of Sulinis is not
to be afcertained; but the form and complications of the
letters in the infcription. are fuch as prevailed about the
time of the former Emperor, that is, towards the clofe of
the fecond century.

[1] Adverfus Britannos quidem Calpurnius Agricola—Capitol. in Vit: Scrip:
Hift: Aug: p. 169.

NUMBER

No. V.

NUMBER V.

DEÆ SULINI PRO SALUTE ET INCOLUMITATE AUFIDII
MAXIMI LEGIONIS VIᵀᴬ VICTRICIS MILITIS AUFI-
DIUS EJUS LEBERTUS *(pro libertus)* VOTUM SOLVIT
LIBENS MERITO.

THIS votive altar exhibits another example of the gratitude and piety of the Romans. It was erected by a
manumitted flave, in performance of a vow made to the
Goddefs Sulinis, for the reftoration of his mafter, who had
made him free.

Luxury, of every fort, was carried to a proverbial
height by this auguft nation. But in no article were the
Romans more extravagantly profufe, than in the ufe of
flaves; and in the multitudes which every citizen of property affected to entertain.—The numerous and various
offices in their town refidences, and country villas; in their

I 2   gardens,

gardens, farms, and fields, were filled by thefe unfortunate beings ; over whom the lordly mafter domineered with the moft uncontrouled and difcretionary fway.[1] To fuch a pitch, indeed, did this vain and cruel cuftom arive, that inftances are not wanting of a noble Roman poffeffing a body of ten, and even twenty thoufand domeftic flaves.[2] Nor was it at home alone that they manifefted this folly; whole troops of thefe wretched men followed them whercever they went; whether to the courts of juftice, or the fenate-houfe; the theatre, the temple, or the bath; *ubi, comitantibus fingulos quinquaginta miniftris tholos introierent balnearum.*[3]—*Familiarium agmina, tanquam predatorios globos, poft terga trahentes; ne Sannione quidem, ut ait Comicus, domi relicto;*[4] and Horace records Tigellinus as parading the ftreets of Rome with a retinue of two hundred fervi at his heels.[5]

---

1 The numbers of flaves employed by the Romans in their kitchens, and about their perfons, muft aftonifh even the moft extravagant of our prefent beaus and epicures.—" Quam celebres culinæ funt ? Quanta nepotum focos juventus premit. " Tranfeo puerorum infelicium greges, quos, poft tranfacta convivia, alii cubiculi " contumeliæ expectant. Tranfeo agmina exoletorum, per nationes colorefque de- " fcripta ut eadem omnibus levitas fit, eadem primæ menfura lanuginis eadem " fpecies capillorum, ne quis, cui rectior eft coma, crifpulis mifceatur. Tranfeo " piftorum turbam, tranfeo miniftratorum per quos, figno dato, ad inferendam cænam " difcurritur. Dii boni!" (Subjoins the philofopher) " quantum hominum " unius Venter exercet." Seneca's Epift :

2 Μυρίας, και δισμυρίας, (οικετας) και ετι πλειυς οι παμπαλλοι κεκτυνται. ουκ επι προσοδοις η, ωσπερ ο των Ελληνων ξεπλυτης Νικιας; αλλ' α πλευς των Ρωμαιων συμπεριιοντας εχουσι των ελευςυς-Athenæus Dæip: Lib: vi.

3 Ammianus, Lib. xxviii.

4 Id: Lib. xiv.

5 Hor: Sat: Lib: 1. 2.

With

With the more humane and reflecting Romans, however, it was not unusual to emancipate their slaves from
this cruel state of bondage, in the cases of faithful service,
and meritorious conduct—This was done by various modes ;
any one of which converted the *Servus* into a *Libertus*, and
though it did not confer on him all the rights and privileges
of Roman citizenship, liberated him notwithstanding, for-
ever, from the tyranny of a passionate, or the caprice of
a whimsical lord.—The only compliment due on this occasion from the manumitted slave to his quondam master,
was to adopt his name; a circumstance which, we perceive
by our inscription, had not been omitted by the freed man
of Aufidius Maximus.

The Sixth legion, mentioned on this altar, was tranf-
ported into Britain, in the time of Hadrian; and probably
accompanied that Emperor, when he took this kingdom in
the tour of his dominions.[1] Its first station was some-
where in the North of England, in the neighbourhood of
the Vallum, the West end of which it appears to have
erected.—Towards the middle of the reign of Antoninus
Pius, it moved rather more to the South, and became
stationary at York.—Here it continued till the beginning
of the fifth century ; when it returned to Italy, to assist in
supporting the sinking fabric of the empire.[2]

---

1 This we have reason to conclude, from the following infcription on an altar,
given by Gale.—" Imperatoris Divi Hadriani ab actis tribuno militum legionis
" fextæ victricis cum qua ex Germaniâ in Britaaniam transiit." Galei Anton:
Itin : p. 47.

2 Horfley's Brit : Rom : 79, 80,

There

There is no room to fuppofe the Legion itfelf was ever at Bath; but from two infcriptions having been found there, in which mention of it occurs, a reafonable conjecture arifes, that one of its difperfed cohorts might have been, at leaft for a time, quartered in this city.

This altar was found on the fcite of the prefent Pump-room, about four years fince.

I have added a reprefentation of the *Focus* or *Thuribulum* on the top of the altar; a cavity intended to receive the libations and frankincenfe offered to the Deity to whom it was dedicated.

NUMBER

I AE · SV
PRO SALVT ET
INCO LAMITA
TE MAR AVFID
MAXIMI · LEG
II · VIC
AVFIDIVS EVA
T AE · HES · LIB
V · S · L · M

Nr. VI.

NUMBER VI.

━━━◖◗◖◗◖◗◖ ◐ ◗◖◗◖◗◖━━━

DEÆ SULINI PRO SALUTE ET INCOLUMITATE MARCI
AUFIDII MAXIMI LEGIONIS VI^{TÆ} VICTRICIS AUFI-
DIUS EJUS ADOPTATUS HERES LEBERTUS VOTUM
SOLVIT LIBENS MERITO.

THE ſtyle of this inſcription; the form of the letters ;
the dimenſions of the altar; together with its being found
on the ſame ſpot, and bearing the ſame names with the laſt ;
lead me to conclude, that it is nearly contemporaneous
with it.—It ſeems to have been erected by the ſame Libertus, probably a ſhort time after the former, when his
patron had conferred the additional favor of adopting
him for his heir and ſucceſſor.—This was not an unuſual
practice with the Romans, for as the law gave them the moſt
unreſtrained diſpoſition of their own property,¹ the limi-

---

¹ It was a law of the twelve tables. " Uti quiſque legaſſit ſuæ rei, ita jus
" eſto."—on which words Pomponius obſerves; " Verbis Legis duodecim tabula-
" rum his uti quiſque legaſſit ſuæ rei, ita jus eſto : latiſſima poteſtas tributa videtur,
" et hæredis inſtituendi, et legata et libertates dandi, tutelas quoque conſtituendi.
" Unde liquet eam ad manumiſſiones etiam pertinere, ut quotquot e ſuis quiſque
" ſervis liberos relinquere vellet, poſſet."—De. verb: Signif: in Verb : Legatis.

tation

tation of it to a favorite flave, who had rendered himfelf ufeful to his mafter; who had flattered his paffions, or humoured his weakneffes, would be natural, and confequently frequent — More particularly, when the teftator had neither confort nor offspring to inherit after him; which was generally the cafe with the Roman foldier; who feldom entered the married ftate till he had compleated his term of military fervice.

NUMBER

No. VII.

NUMBER VII.

PEREGRINUS SECUNDI FILIUS CIVIS TREVERIS JOVI
CETIO MARTI ET NEMETONA VOTUM SOLVIT LI-
BENS MERITO.

THIS votive altar was difcovered feveral feet under
ground, in the year one thoufand feven hundred and fifty-
four, in the upper part of Stall-ftreet. It is dedicated to
three deities, the Cetian Jupiter, Mars, and Nemetona.

The name of the perfon who erected it does not appear,
for the word *Peregrinus* is merely an appellative; implying
that he was a ftranger or traveller.[1]—We find, however,
by the fecond and third lines, the name of his father, Se-
cundus ; and the city of his refidence, Treves in Germany.

Though it be fufficiently evident from the writings of
the more enlightened and philofophic Romans, that they
were Deifts, and held the wild and abfurd notions of Polytheifm in fecret contempt, yet the belief of a multiplicity

[1] Amongft the Romans it was extremely common for perfons to receive names
from certain circumftances of their birth or fortune ; fuch as *Vopifcus*, an appellation
given to the furvivor of two twins, when one died in parturition ; *Cæfar*, *Agrippa*,
and others.

K   of

of deities tainted the popular mind, and pervaded all the
middle and lower orders of the empire.¹ Error being once
admitted, increased in a rapid degree; and bewildered
reason not satisfied with erecting every element, paffion,
and even abstracted idea, into a divinity ; taught at length,
that there were a variety of Gods of the fame name, differ-
ing, however, in their acts and characters.

This was the cafe more particularly with the greater
deities; and there was fcarcely a town, of any confequence, throughout the Roman empire, which had not its
peculiar Jove, Minerva, or Mars. Thefe differed not
only in their characters, but in their reprefentations alfo;²
and fo materially, that the Jove of Terracina, or Jupiter
Anxur, was fculptured with the beautiful and beardlefs
face of the fon of Maia, or the brother of Latona, inftead
of the awful countenance, of the father of Gods and men.³

It was to a local Jupiter of this kind, the peculiar God
of the municipal town, Cetium,⁴ in Germany, (together
with Mars and Nemetona) that this altar was dedicated.

1 Omnes gentes una lex, et fempiterna, et immortalis, continebit; unufque
erit, quafi magifter, et imperator omnium, Deus. Cicero : Frag :'Lib : 3. De Repub.
2 Montfaucon, Tom. 1. Plate 12. Fig. 9.
 3 Bis fex cæleftes, medio Jove, fedibus altis
 Auguftâ gravitate fedent. Sua quemque deorum
 Infcribit facies: Jovis eft regalis Imago.
                              Ov : Met : l. 6. v. 74.
4 Norici oppid Anton : Baudrando Pagus Auftriæ inferioris ad Danubium, ubi
recipit Anzefpach Amnem. Hoffmanni Lex : Tom : i. p.1. Municipii dig-
ritatem, non coloniæ literati lapides urbi contribreunt.—Fuit Municipium ad Mon-
tem Kalenberg. Anton : Itin : apud Weffelin : p. 234. Now called Kotwig:
Simp : in Id.

The

The laſt of theſe deities ſeems to have been a Britiſh one, and known only in the South-Weſtern parts of England.— The name Nemetotacio (which Baxter confiders as ſynonymous with Nemetomagus) ſeems in the chorography of Anonymous Ravennas,[1] and is conjectured, by Baxter, to be the preſent Launceſton.[2]— If this be allowed, the near approach of Nemetona to the town Nemetomagus, will juſtify the opinion of the former being the local divinity of the latter.

1 Horſley, p. 490.
2 Bax: Gloſſ: Antiq: p. 172. 182.

SVLEVIS
SVLINVS
SCVLTOR
BRVCE· I · I
V· S· L· M· P· I · I·

No. VIII.

NUMBER VIII.

SULEVIS SULINUS SCULTOR *(pro fculptor)* BRUCETI
FILIUS SACRUM FECIT LIBENS MERITO.

THIS altar was found at the fame time and place with
the one laft-defcribed. It is dedicated to the *Suliva*, the
Deæ campeftres; or local rural deities of the country
around Bath;

> *Sunt ruftica numina Nymphæ*
> *Faunique, Satyrique, et Monticolæ Sylvani.*[1]

A con-

---

1 Ovid: Met: Lib: i. v. 192. Thefe were inferior intelligences to the *Dii ruftici*,
who more immediately prefided over *Agriculture*, and affifted the labours of the
hufbandman. Varro invokes, and enumerates thefe deities in the beginning of his
work *Re ruftica.* " Quoniam, ut ajunt, Dei facientes adjuvant, prius invocabo
eos; nec ut Homerus, et Ennius *Mufas:* fed xii. *Deos confentes.* Neque tamen
Urbanos, quorum imagines ad forum auratæ ftant, fex mares et totidem fæminæ, fed
illos xii. Deos, qui maxime agricolarùm duces funt. Primum, qui omnes fructus
agriculturæ cælo et terra continent, *Jovem* et *Tellurem*; itaque duo hi parentes
magni

A conjecture that is confiderably firengthened by the magnitude and depth of its Focus, which is well calculated to receive the abundant offering of herbs, fruits, and flowers, with which thefe fancied intelligences were fuppofed to be pleafed.

The aukward form, and bad fculpture of this altar, place its execution at a time when the arts were fadly degenerated here; probably not long before the Romans quitted Britain.

magni dicuntur : *Jupiter* pater appellatur : *Tellus* terra mater. Secundo *Solem* et *Lunam*, quorum tempora obfervantur, cum quædam feruntur et conduntur. Tertio *Cererem* et *Liberum*, quod horum fructus maxime neceffarii ad victum. Ab his enim cibus et potio venit è fundo. Quarto, *Robigus* ac *Floram*, quibus propitiis, neque *rubigo* frumenta, neque arbores corrumpit, neque non tempeftive floreat. Itaque publicè *Robigo* ferix, *Robigalia*, *Floræ* ludi *Floralia* inftituti. Item advenero *Minervam* et *Venerem*, quarum unius procuratio *Oliveti*, alterius hortorum : quo nomine ruftica Vinalia inftituta. Nec non etiam precor *Lympham* et *Bonum Eventum*; quoniam fine aquâ omnis arida ac mifera *agricultura*; fine *facceffu* ac bono eventu; fruftratio eft, non cultura."

No. IX.

NUMBER IX,

LOCUM RELIGIOSUM PER INSOLENTIAM FRUTUM
VIRTUTE INAUGURATUM REPURGATUM P⸱ IDIDIT
CAIUS SEVERIUS EMERITUS CENTURIO POSUIT ERGO
GRATIÆ.

THIS monumental *Cippus* was found in Stall ſtreet, on
the 29th of June, 1753. It commemorates the re-edifica-
tion of ſome place of worſhip, which had fallen into difuſe
and decay. Caius Severius Emeritus,¹ a centurion, re-
ſtored, and dedicated it afreſh; and erected the above
ſtone in teſtimony of this act of piety. The centurial
mark (which is nothing more than the inverted initial of
Centurio), being of the ſhape much in uſe about the
middle of the fourth century, enables us to form ſome idea
of the antiquity of this Cippus.

---

1 If the word *Emeritus* be taken for an appellative inſtead of a Cognomen, it will
mean a *Veteran*; or one who had completed his years of ſervice, and received his
diſcharge. " Emeriti dicuntur Veterani, ſolutique milites, qui jam in uſu prælii
" nou ſunt, quia mereri militare dicuntur, a ſtipendiis ſcilicet, quæ merentur.
" Iidem et veterani dicuntur, quia jam in uſu prælii non ſunt ſeu, poſt multos mi-
" litiæ labores quietis ſuffragium conſequuntur." Valirin: de Re Mil: Rom: vi 5.

No. X.

A

B

NUMBER X.

WHAT the original ufe or defign of this ftone might have been, it is now difficult to fay. It appears to be part of a fculpture exhibiting a military commander in pretty bold relief. From the rudely-chiffel'd dolphin on the left hand corner, it fhould feem that a *naval officer* was intended to be reprefented; fince that fifh was confidered facred to Neptune,[1] and held to be an emblem of extenfive maritime power;[2]

Οὐδε μαἰην παλαμαις χατεχα Δελφινα και κιθῶ :
Τη μεν γαρ γαιαν, τη δε θαλαττα εχει.[3]

In matters, which, (from particular circumftances), will not admit of demonftration, it may be allowable to advance

---

[1] " Qui Neptuno fimulacrum faciunt, Delphinum aut in manu ejus, aut fub pede " conftituere videntur; quod gratiffimum Neptuno effe arbitrantur."—Hyginus in Delphino.

[2] Vet: Græc: Epig: in Anthol: on a Cupid holding a flower in one hand and a dolphin in the other.

L   rational

rational conjecture in the room of proof.—Prefuming upon this privilege, I would venture to offer an opinion that the ftone under confideration, might have been erected to the honor of Caraufius, a bold ufurper in the reign of Dioclefian, who, by his confummate gallantry, and extraordinary naval fkill, obtained the compleat dominion of Britain and held it for feven years. The following account of him is given by Eutropius. " Caraufius, though " very meanly born, obtained a confiderable poft in " the army, and acquired a great reputation, whilft he " enjoyed it. He at Bononia received a commiffion to " keep all quiet at fea upon the Belgic and Armorican " coaft, infefted by the Franks and Saxons; and having " taken many of the barbarians, without either returning " the whole booty to the provincials, or remitting the " fame to the Emperors ; a fufpicion arofe, that he de- " fignedly fuffered the Barbarians to make inroads that he " might catch them as they were going off with their booty, " and by thefe means enrich himfelf. Orders were given " to Maximian to kill him; upon which he affumed the " purple, and feized on Britain; and when force had been " ufed in vain, they were glad at laft to ftrike up a peace " with him. Seven years afterwards, he was killed by " Alectus his companion, who himfelf kept poffeffion of " Britain for three years after the death of Caraufius, and " then was fuppreffed by the management of Afclepio- " dotus, the Captain of the guards."[1]

1 Horfley's Brit: Rom: p. 69.

Sculptural

Sculptural reprefentations of their great men, were, we know, very cuftomary modes of flattery amongft the Romans, particularly under the lower empire, when altars, ftatues, and temples were raifed, and divinity attached to the poffeffion of the purple, however vicious or contemptible the wearer might be. Many fuch compliments would doubtlefs be paid to the fuccefsful ufurper *Caraufus*, and as the ftyle of fculpture obfervable in the ftone before us, marks it to have been chiffelled when the arts were on the decline, this, (together with other circumftances) feems to juftify the opinion of its having been, originally, a reprefentation of him.

The drefs of the figure, alfo, is that of a military commander; a loofe cloak, called a *Chlamys*, which covered the clofer veft, or *Tunica*, and was faftened on the right fhoulder with a *Fibula*, or clafp. The *Dolphin*, moreover, points at the fame profeffion; being a fymbol of activity and difpatch, and therefore a very proper accompaniment to a fculpture of this kind. The coins of Vefpafian, (who affected the motto of Auguftus, σπεῦδε Βρᾳδέως;) very frequently exhibit on their reverfes, the Dolphin entwined with an anchor; to denote expedition and alacrity, coupled, at the fame time, with prudence and moderation.

It is to be remarked further, that the cropped hair, and fhort curling beard, obfervable in this relief, befpeak a foldier of the lower empire; when it became fafhionable

to

wear the laſt appendage to the face.[1] The hiſtory of *beards*
indeed, amongſt the Romans is ſomewhat ſingular, and
well exemplifies the caprice and mutable nature of faſhion.
In the early ages of the commonwealth, whilſt the Roman
character continued to be a ſerious one, the *beard* was
carefully cheriſhed, and regarded with veneration;[2] nor
were barbers heard of in the capital of the world, till
four hundred and fifty years after its foundation, when
they were firſt introduced there by *Ticinius Mœna* from
Sicily.[3] What ceaſes to be faſhionable, however, ſoon

---

1 It was a cuſtom with the Romans to crop the hair ſhort in the neck, when they
aſſumed the *Toga virilis*, at the age of ſeventeen; and to keep it ever after in the
ſame ſtate—This was done with great ſolemnity, and the ſhorn locks were generally
offered to ſome deity or other—Frequently to Bacchus;

Ille genas Phæbo, crinem hic paſcebat Jaccho.
Statius Theb: 8. 492.

Sometimes to Apollo:

Accipe laudatos juvenis Phæbeie crines
Quos tibi Cæſareus donat puer, accipe lætûs,
Intonſoque oſtende patri.
Stat: lib: 3. Sil: 4.

At other times to Jove;

Jupitér hunc crinem, voti reus, ante dicarem.
Si pariter nati virides libare dediſſes
Ad tua templa genas——

2 Livy Lib: v.—41.—

Lucan alſo deſcribes *Cato*, as rigidly obſerving the faſhion of the beard;

Intonſos rigidam in frontem deſcendere canos
Paſſus erat, mæstamque genis in creſcere barbam. Lib. 2.

3. Pliny, Lib: vii. c. 59. Omnino tonſores in Italiam ex Sicilia primum
veniſſe dicuntur, poſt Romam conditam Anno Quadringenteſimo quinquageſimo
quarto, ut ſcriptum in publico Ardea in literis extat, eoſque adduxiſſe P. Ticinium
Menam. M: Varro de Re Ruſt: Lib: 2. Cap; ult.

begins

begins to be confidered as abfurd. The refined Romans adopting the oriental cuftom of fhaving the chin, quickly loft all refpect for their ancient cuftom, and laughed heartily at the fimplicity of their anceftors, in following one that was now termed barbarous and ridiculous ;

Credam dignum Barbá, dignumq Capillis
Majorum.[1]

The Beard became a fubject of fcorn wherever it appeared ; and the poor philofopher's chin fuffered many a practical joke from the mifchievous urchins of the Auguftan age :

Vellent tibiBa rbam
Lafcivi pueri.[2]

Inconftant fafhion, however, rendered the beard once more refpectable, and Hadrian, in the beginning of the fecond century, again gave it popularity, by encouraging the growth of his own.[3] Succeeding Emperors followed his example; and the cuftom kept its ground, till the termination of the empire.[4]

The

---

1 Juv : Sat : 16. 3ª.
2 Hor : Sat : Lib : 1. Sat : 3. v. 134.
3 Αδριανۛ πρωτۛ γιναι καϊϣηξι. Xiphilin : in vit : Trajani :   'Γεγεννγ.
4 The Hiftory of Beards in our own country, would well difplay the inftability of fafhion, if the fubject were worth purfuing ; it may be remarked, however, by the bye, that Henry the 1ft, was the firft who introduced fhaving into England, as we

are

The two fragments A. and B. are probably ornaments
of a portal.—The former seems to have a particular reference to Bath.—I take it to be part of the figure of a
Genius, holding a *Strigil* in his right hand ; an inftrument
of brafs, iron, or filver, with which the attendants at the
Baths, cleanfed the bodies of the bathers.[1]—The latter
fragment belonged to the reprefentation of another Genius, who patronized rural employments ; and delighted
in the fruits of the earth, and the flowers of the field ;

Tellurem porco, Silvanum lacte piabant,
Floribus et vino Genium, memorem brevis ævi.[2]

Thefe fubordinate intelligences make a confiderable figure
in claffical mythology, and confequently deferve a moment's
attention.—Various were the opinions of the ancients
refpecting them. Plutarch confiders them as intermediate
beings between the Gods and men.[3] Varro, as the mental
or intellectual part of man.[4] Others as the tutelary Deities
of ftates, cities, and individuals.[5] Some fancied thefe imaginary

are informed.—" Henricus comam in hac infula princeps barbamque totondit,
ejusque exemplo ducti Angli qui a fumma memoria capillo promiffo fuerant, omnes
confeftim tondebantur." Theod : Clainus Hiftor : Britan : Lib : 3.

1 Sanadon's Note in Hor : Sat : Lib : 2. 7. v. 109.

2 Hor : Epift : 11, Ep : 1. v. 143.

3 Το των δαιμονων γενος εν μεσω θεων κ ανθρωπων : de Orac.

4 " Genium effe uniufcujufque animum rationalem et ideo effe fingulos fingulorum."
Varro apud Aurel : Auguftin.

5 " Genium Dicebant antiqui naturalem Deum, uniufcujufque loci, vel rei, aut
hominis." Servius in 1mo. Georgic. Virgilii. " Suus cuique mos, fuus cuique
ritus

ginary beings were two in number, which took charge of every perfon from the moment of his nativity, one of whom continually impelled him to good, the other to evil.[1] That they were conftantly employed in this beneficial or pernicious work, and never quitted him for a moment of time, from his birth to his deceafe.[2] Having this powerful influence over human actions, and temporal affairs, the *Genii* were held in profound veneration, and divine honors paid to them, both by ftates and individuals. Various offerings were efteemed to be agreeable to them. A pig of two months old;

> *Cras Genium mero*
> *Curabis et porco bimeftri.*[3]

A falted cake;

> *Tu cefpile vivo*
> *Ponefocum, Geniumque loci Faunumque Laremque*
> *Salfo farre voca.*[4]

ritus eft, varios cuftodes urbibus cunctis mens divina difiribuit, ut animæ nafcenti-
bus, ita populis fatales Genii dividuntur." Q: Symnachus in Relatione fua al
A. A. A. pro reftaurando Deorum gentilium Cultu.

1 Cum nafcimur duos Genios fortimur, unus eft, qui hortatur ad Bona ; alter qui
depravat ad mala, nec incongrue dicuntur *Genii*, quia cum unufquifque genitus fuerit
ei ftatim obfervatores deputantur; quibus affiftentibus poft mortem aut aflerimur in
meliorem vitam aut condemnimur in deteriorem." Servius in hoc Virgilii."
" Quifque fuos patimur manes."

2 Genius autem ita nobis affiduos obfervator appofitus eft, ut ne puncto quidem
temporis longius abfcedat, fed ab utero matris exceptos ad extremum vitæ diem
comitetur. Cenforin : de die Natal : c. 3.
Απαντι δαιμων ανδρι τω γινμενω. Menander,
Omni homini nafcenti Genius,

3 Hor : Od : Lib : 3. 17.
4 Calphurn : Sic : Ec : 5.

An

An oblation of Frankincenfe ;

Magne Geni, cape thura libens, votifque faveto ;
Si modo cum de me cogitat ille cadet.[1]

Fruits and wine ; or wine alone ;
Funde merum Genio.[2]

Thefe offerings were generally made on the natal day of the pious votary, in a private manner, in his own manfion. But to the *Genius* of every particular ftate or city, a temple was raifed at the public expence, and divine rites publicly obferved on particular days fet apart for that purpofe,[3]

---

1 Tibullus, Lib: 4. de Natali Cerinthi,
2 A: Perfius in princip : Sat: 6.
3 In Rome, in the 14th Region of the city, was a chapel dedicated *ad Genii liberorum*; another, *ad Genios Larium*, in the 6th Region ; and a third, in the 7th, *ad Genium Sangi.*—Rofinus Antiquitat : Rom: Lib: 2. c. xiv. Ammianus Marcellinus mentions a temple to the fame intelligence in Alexandria. Lib: 22.

NUMBER

Fig. XI.

NUMBER XI,

────────

IT is fomewhat fingular, that a very intelligent and refpectable antiquary of the prefent day, fhould have miftaken the monument before us, for the production of the Saxon or Gothic age; when its form, fubject, and every other circumftance, manifeft it to be intimately connected with claffical mythology.[1]—The fculpture, indeed, is not remarkable for elegance, having been executed, (as I fhall prefently fhew) towards the beginning of the fourth century, when the arts were very much on the decline; but, perhaps, we can fcarcely judge now, fairly, of its original execution, fince it is worked on Bath ftone, the friable nature of which, prevents the long prefervation of the finer and minuter parts of any piece of fculpture.

Amongft the ancients it was an ufual practice to dedicate the *fame temple* to feveral deities.—Thus Hercules and the Mufes were joined in one at Rome; as well as Caftor and

---

[1] Governor Pownal's " Defcriptions and Explanations of fome Remains of " Roman Antiquities dug up in the City of Bath ;" p: 56.

M   Pollux:

Pollux; Pan and Ceres; Apollo and Æſculapius.—Thoſe
alſo, who in their attributes bore any reſemblance to each
other, were often aſſociated together upon *the ſame altar.*
When this occurred, the divinities were called Συμβωμιοι
and ὁμοβωμιοι, and the altars themſelves Διβωμοι, or double
altars.—Of this ſort was the one before us, which appears
to have been dedicated to *Jupiter* and *Hercules bibax,* or
the convivial Hercules.[1] The following explanation of
the two figures will probably be conſidered as ſufficient
proofs of the truth of this opinion.

The left-hand relief repreſents *Jupiter* with thoſe various
emblems which diſtinguiſh him from the other deities of
ancient mythology.

[1] In the frequent Lectiſterniums which the Romans made to Hercules, they uſed
even to invoke him under his *drunken character,* as one finds by *Statius;* and a particular friend of that poet had a very remarkable little figure of this God, which he
uſed to place upon his table, whenever any gaieties were carrying on there. He
held a cyathus in one hand, and his club in the other, with a mild good-humoured
look, that ſeemed to invite others to be as happy and well pleaſed as himſelf.—
Spence's Polymetis, p. 126.

> Nec torva effigies, epuliſque aliena remiffis;
> Sed qualem parci domus admirata Molorchi,
> Aut Aleæ lucis vidit Tegeæa ſacerdos :
> Qualis et Oetæis emiſſus in Aſtra favillis
> Nectar adhuc torvâ lætus Junone bibebat.
> Sic mitis vultus; veluti de pectore gaudens
> Hortetur menſas. Tenet hæc marcentia fratris
> Pocula; adhuc ſævæ meminit manus altera pugnæ ;
> Suſtinet occultum Nemeæo tegmine Saxum.
> Statius Sylv: 6. v. 58.

The

(59)

The God grafps in his right-hand, the *fulmen*, lightning, or three-forked bolt, according to the defcriptions of the poet ;

Cui dextra trifulcis
Ignibus armata eft.[1]

With his left he holds his fceptre, as the King or father of all beings, whether human or divine ;

Celfior ipfe loco, fceptroque innixus eburno.[2]

At his feet may be feen the " feathered king," or eagle ; which from its fuperiority to other birds, was confidered as the peculiar attendant on Jove, and the bearer of his lightning ;

Magni Jovis ales fertur in altum
Affueto volitans, geftes ceu fulmina Mundi.[3]

The head and countenance are much mutilated, but fufficient of the former remains to teftify that it was originally modelled, in the circumftances of the hair, beard, &c. after the fublime defcription given by Homer, of the father of Gods and men ;

Η, και κυανεησιν επ' οφρυσι νευσε Κρονιων ;
Αμβροσιαι δ'αρα χαιται επερρωσανθο ανακθος,
Κρατος απ' αθανατοιο· μεγαν δ' ελελιξεν Ολυμπον.[4]

1 Ov: Met: L. 2, v. 325.   2 Id: Lib: 1. v. 178.   3 Manilius, Lib: 1. v. 345.
4 Hom: Il : L: 1, v. 521.

His

His only covering is a regal *Pallium.* thrown over the left fhoulder, and hanging loofely around the body.—— The figure which occupies the other face of this bifronted altar, is the reprefentation of *Hercules Bibax,* or the convivial Hercules.

The ufual attributes of this deity were his lion's fkin, club, and bow ;

      Ουκ Ηρακλης ητος εστιν ; ημηνην αλλ⊙-, μα τον Ηρακλεα το τοξον, το ροπαλον, η λεοντη, το μεγεθος.[1]

The two former of which are fufficiently vifible in the relief.

But when he was reprefented under his drunken character, inflead of the latter implement of war, he bore in his right hand a *cyathus,* or goblet——

        ——*Tenet hæc marcentia fratris*
    Pocula,[2]

This emblem was given him, in allufion both to his intemperate propenfities, and alfo to a wild mythological fable, which feigned that he traverfed the ocean in a *Scyphus* or drinking veffel; a ftory that had its rife, accord-

<hr/>

[1] Lucian, tom: 1, p. 298.
[2] Statius ut fupra.

                                   ing

ing to Macrobius, from a voyage performed by this
adventurous hero, not in a goblet, but in a small ship, that
bore the name of *Scyphus.*[1]

The affociation of *Jove* and *Hercules* on the fame altar,
was not unufual; inftances of it occur in Gruter and
Montfaucon. The practice, however, flourifhed more particularly during the joint reign of Dioclefian and Maxi-
minian; the former of whom affected the name and character of Jove, the latter thofe of Hercules.[2] This circumftance may be confidered as an index to the date of our
altar, which was probably raifed to the honor of thefe
Emperors; and places it confequently, fomewhere between
the years of our Lord 284. and 304, a period which
comprehends the term of their dominion over the Roman
empire.[3]

This altar feems to have filled the corner of fome temple;
two of its fides being rough and unwrought.—Its focus
was evidently intended to receive libations and offerings.

1 Macrob: Saturn: L. 5. c. 21.

2. Jupiter et Hercules nonnunquam occurrunt cum hoc titulo *Dii Magni.*—Hæc
Jovi et Herculi fimul oblata religio maxime vigebat ævo Diocletiani et Maximiani,
quorum prior *Jovius,* fecundus *Herculius* in honorem duorum horumce numinum
vocitatus eft.—Montfaucon, tom: 1. p. 47.

3 Eutropius, Lib: ix, c, 22.

No. XII.

NUMBER XII.

AT the time of difcovering the two preceding pieces of fculpture, this curious fragment was alfo dug up. It feems to have been the pediment of a fmaller temple, chapel, or *facellum*, dedicated probably to the Goddefs *Luna*, under one of her various names and characters.[1]— The head which appears in the centre, is executed in rude, but bold relief; and exhibits a broad Ethiopian countenance, with the hair dreffed in very large curls; and tied at the top in a knot.—A crefcent encircles it; and a knotted wand, with a ferpent twifting round it, appears on the right fide, without the crefcent.

That this fpecimen of antique mafonry originally made part of an edifice dedicated to the intelligence which was fuppofed to prefide over the moon, will probably appear from the following remarks.

[1] Cicero enumerates fome of her appellations, and gives the reafons for their being applied to her. Cic: de Nat: Deor: 2. n 68.

The

The Greeks and Romans borrowing their mythological and philofophical notions from the Egyptians, adopted the tenet of the eternity of the fun and moon,[1] and confidered thefe planets as the great parents of univerfal life, the authors and fupporters of animated nature;

αλλα γονηων
Παντων ζωοντων, οις αμφιθαλης ετι φυτλη.[2]

Numerous temples were erected to them individually, throughout the empire; and at Rome, no lefs than three, with a fmall chapel, flood dedicated to the fair planet of the night.[3] The moft confiderable of thefe was fituate on the Aventine mount;

Aventino Luna colenda jugo ;[4]

And here, under the name of *Noctiluca*, the moon received divine honors.

But the worfhip of this planet was not confined to the city of Rome alone. It found its way into all the colonies and provinces; and as the influence and powers of the

---

f 1 Υπολαβειν (Egyptii) ειναι δυο θευς αιδιυς τον τε ηλιον και την σεληνην. Diod. Sic: Αιγια σημαινοντες ηλιον και σεληνην γραφυσι, δια το αιωνια ειναι ςοιχεια. Hor: Apol : in Ιεςογλυφ :
2 Sibyllina Carmina, apud Zofim : Hiftor : L, 2.
3 Dempfter's Antiq. Rom : p. 165.
4 Ov : Faft : L. 3. in fin.

moon were esteemed to be various and important, so her worship was cultivated with the most rigid care and attention.—Constant fires illuminated her temples during the night; and particular sacrifices marked the different stages of her appearance; her increase, her full, and wane. When her countenance was obscured with clouds, or hidden by an eclipse, various ceremonies were observed to court her re-appearance, or to relieve her from the effects of those witcheries, by which the wild wanderings of Heathen superstition esteemed her, in the latter case, to be oppressed.

> *Candida nec magicas artes, inimicaque verba*
> *Passa, nec a radiis terræ molimine fratris*
> *Intercepta sui, bissenas Delia noctes*
> *Horruit, et fusca texit caligine vultum.*
> *——Quantum pavidæ succurrere Lunæ*
> *Certantes populi tinnitibus æris acuti*
> *Ingeminant, surdasque Deæ nituntur ad aures*
> *Thessalicum ne carmen eat, detractaque cælo*
> *Suppositas lato terras simul obruat orbe,*[1]

The influence of this planet, also, over the human frame was considered as very powerful, and in several diseases it was customary to invoke the moon for cure or relief.

---

1 Pet: Apollon : Collatis de Excidio Hierosolym. Lib: 1,

From

From this circumſtance more eſpecially, it ſeems probable, that a temple or *Sacellum* to the Goddeſs *Luna*, might be erected in the Roman colony of *Aquæ Solis*; ſince it was hither that the afflicted invalids, from all parts of the kingdom, reſorted, to recruit their ſtrength, and regain their health; and nothing is more likely, than that an intelligence efficacious in reſtoring bodily vigor, ſhould be worſhipped on a ſpot where her influence was more particularly known and experienced.— Indeed the emblem which ſurrounds the head, in this piece of ſculpture, ſeems to prove beyond diſputation, that the edifice to which it belonged, had a particular referrence to the *Moon*. For in almoſt all the ancient ſculptures, and on the reverſes of moſt of the coins, which repreſent this intelligence under a corporeal form, the emblem of a lunar crown, or a creſcent, accompanies her, and points out the

Siderum Regina bicornis—,[1]
" The Queen of Stars who rules the night,
" In horned Majeſty of light.[2]

The ſerpent twining itſelf round the ſtick with a knot on its top, is a very proper ornament, alſo, for a temple erected to a deity ſuppoſed to be influential in removing bodily complaints; ſince it is an emblem of Æſculapius, the God of healing and convaleſcence. In the pharma-

---

[1] Hor: Carm: Sec: L : 35.
[2] Francis's Hor: v. 2. p. 301.

copera of antiquity, the fnake was in conftant ufe, and a
variety of good effects were attributed to it.[1]—Hence it
became facred to Æfculapius, whofe reprefentation is
generally accompanied by the figure of a ferpent. The
knotted ftick adumbrates the difficulty attending the practice
of phyfic;[2] and both together form an appropriate
emblem of the perfonage who invented the art, and commanded the means of reftoring health and vigor.[3] It is by
this accompaniment that the God, in the language of the
poet, defcribes himfelf to be diftinguifhed ;

Pone metus; veniam; fimulacraque noftra relinquam,
Hunc modo ferpentem, baculum qui nexibus ambit ;
Perfpice et ufque nota.[4]

And Apulicius mentions it as the circumftance by which
his reprefentation may be cafieft known ;

Diceres Dei medici baculo, quod ramulis femiamputatis nodo-
fum gerit, ferpentem generofum lubricis amplexibus inhærere.[5]

---

[1] Quin et inefle ei (angui) remedia multa creduntur, et ideo Efculapio dicatur.—
Plin : Nat : Hift : Lib : 29.

[2] Bacillum habet (Æfculapius) nodofum, quod difficultatem fignificat artis.—
Teft : Pomp: Lib : 9°.

[3] Ασκληπιον
Ηξια παντοδαπαν αλικτηξα ιηται. Pindar, Pythior : ode 3.

[4] Ov : Met : 15. 662.

[5] L. : Apul : Lib : 1mo. Mile ; in principio.

N U M B E R XIII.

THIS fine bronze head was dug up in the month of July 1727, in Stall-ftreet, where it lay buried fixteen feet under the furface of the ground. It is a beautiful fragment of a ftatue of Apollo, which ftood, probably, in a temple dedicated to him, near the fpot where the head was difcovered.

That this Deity fhould have a temple raifed to his honor, in a city which received its appellation from himfelf, will fcarcely admit of a queftion, particularly as he was efteem-ed to be potent in the infliction and cure of many diforders.

Homer introduces him very fublimely, as defcending from Olympus, and difcharging amongft the Grecians his arrows winged with plague and peftilence.

By

Βη δε κατ' ελυμπιο καρηνων χωομενῷ κηρ,
Τοξ' ωμοισιν εχων, αμφηρεφεα τε φαρετρην·
Εκλαγξαν δ'αρ οϊςοι επ' ωμων χωομενοιο,
Αυτε κινηθενῷ. ΄ο δ' ηϊε νυκτι εοικως.
Εζετ' επειτ' απανευθε νεων, μετα δ'ιον εηκε·
Δεινη δε κλαγγη γενετ' αργυρεοιο βιοιο·
Ουρηας μεν πρωτον επωχελο, και κυνας αργης.
Αυταρ επειτ' αυτοισι βελῷ εχεπευκες εφιεις,
Βαλλ'.[1]

And fhortly after, as removing the malady from their
camp, at the interceffion of his favorite prieft :

Ηδ' ετι και νυν μοι τοδ' επικρηηνον εελδωρ,
Ηδη νυν Δαναοισιν αεικεα λοιγον αμυνον·
Ως εφατ' ευχομενῷ· τα δ' εκλυε φοιβῷ Απολλων.[2]

The *Apollo Mædicus*, or healing Apollo, occurs alfo in
other poets, as the inventor of medicine, and the difcoverer
of the ufe of fimples :

Inventum medicina meum eft ; opiferque per orbem
Dicer ; et Herbarum fubjecta potentia nobis.[3]

The claim of Apollo to this fragment is further ftrengthened, by the circumftance of the *hair*; which curls luxu-

1 Hom: Il: 1. 44.
2 Il: 1. v. 455.
3 Ov: Met; 15. 24.

riantly

riantly round the face, and falls in graceful ringlets behind
the head. This was a ſtriking characteriſtic of the God's
perſon, and procured him, amongſt the Greeks, the appellation ακερσικομης, or long-locked; and with the Romans,
that of *Grannus* or *Grynæus*, a Celtic appellative, deſcriptive
of the radiant, thick, and trembling Solar beams.[1]—To
the flowing locks of Apollo, the poets are perpetually
alluding;

Dignos et Apollini crines,

Says Ovid of a beautiful head of hair: and Tibullus,
in an addreſs to the God himſelf, does not forget to cele-
brate his profuſe ringlets as conſtituting a chief ornament
of his perſon;

Nunc indue veſtem
Sepoſitam, longas nunc bene pecte comas.

On a coin preſerved in the Numiſmata of Albertus
Rubenius,[2] is a reverſe, repreſenting *Apollo conservator*, the

---

1 Grynæus and Grannus are evidently derived from the Celtic *Gri n*; which is
compoſed of *Cri*, trembling, and *Tein*, fire.—In the oblique caſes *Tein* makes *Tien*,
which is pronounced *Ein*, or *Ен*; the conſonants which begin the nominative of
Celtic words being invariably quieſcent in the genitive; ſo that Cri-ein, or Cri-an,
literally ſignifies the *trembling fire*, in alluſion to the Sun's appearance to the eye.—
Offian countenances this etymon of *Grian* in his addreſs to that luminary.—Na en,
oig derfa n'airdian—when thou *trembled* at the gate of the Weſt.—Vide Macpher-
ſon's Int: to the Hiſt: of Great Britain and Ireland, p. 102.

2 Tabula 60. N. 5,

repelle?

repeller of peſtilence and difeaſe, and averter of evil. He there appears crowned with laurel,[1] and bearing a lyre in his hand. As his office in this city was of a ſimilar nature, we may ſuppoſe the ſtatue under conſideration, when perſeƈt, exhibited him in the ſame charaƈter, and with the ſame accompaniment; and ſtanding, probably, in the Penetralia of his own temple, he exemplified, in many particulars, the exquiſitely beautiful deſcription of a picture of this God, given by Tibullus;

Hic juvenis caſtâ redimitus tempora lauro
   Eſt viſus noſtrâ ponere ſede pedem:
Non illo quicquam formoſius ulla priorum
   Ætas, humanum nec videt illud opus.
Intonſi crines longâ cervice fluebant;
   Stillabat Tyrio myrtea rore coma.
Candor erat, qualem præfert Latonia Luna;
   Et color in niveo corpore purpureus:
Ut Juveni primum virgo deduƈta marito
   Inficitur teneras ore rubente genas;
Ut quum contexunt amaranthis alba puellæ
   Lilia, et Autumno candida mala rubent.[2]

---

1 It is evident that ſome ſpecies of ornament encircled the head, as there are ſeveral perforations, by the means of which it appears to have faſtened on.
2 Tibullus, El: Lib: 2.

No. XIV.

NUMBER XIV.

IT is with confiderable diffidence that I enter on the confideration of this piece of antique mafonry; being fo
unfortunate as to differ in opinion refpecting it, with a
gentleman whofe deep erudition and intimate acquaintance
with antiquarian fubjects, render him fo much better qualified than myfelf, for the inveftigation, and illuftration of
whatever is doubtful or obfcure in that line of refearch.
But as no *Hypothefis*, however happy it may be, can amount
to abfolute demonftration; further conjectures on the
fubject, notwithftanding the ingenious remarks of Governor
Pownal, are by no means precluded; and that liberality of
fentiment which ufually accompanies intellectual excellence, will, I truft, require no apology, when I offer fuch
as have arifen in my mind after an attentive confideration of
this curious remain of antiquity.

The Governor's opinion with regard to it will be found
in the following extract from his pamphlet.

The

"The *Symbolic Head*, found in the fame place, which I propofe here to defcribe and to explain, when viewed as we fee it, in its prefent fituation, cut in ftrong and coarfe lines, appears to be a very ordinary rough piece of fculpture ; but when fet in the fituation in which it muft have been placed, two or three and thirty feet high, it would give the proper effect, which, if cut in more delicate lines, it would not have given. It is carved on a mafonry of large ftones,the remaining parts of which, fhew that this mafonry was the Tympanum of a pediment of fome confiderable building.—By what maybe collected from feveral fragments found in the fame place with this, it appears that the veftibule of this building muft have been of a very richCorinthian order, and (allowing for the difference of the Roman and Englifh) about thirty feet fquare in breadth and height ; and that, moft probably, the interior fpace of the temple was a double cube of thefe dimenfions.

"Whoever examines this fymbolic ornament, with deliberate and diftinct ideas, formed on the fact, will difcover that this head is no head of Medufa ;

——*Crinita draconibus ora*, Ov : Met : lib. 4.

"He will not find the hair to be *crines anguicomæ*; he will fee the hair, though rudely cut, remaining *in its natural ftate*. He may obferve the ferpents mixed with the hair *furround* or *are placed upon* the *caput pinnatum*, as fomewhat adfcititious. Two ferpents are tied together in a kind

kind of knot under the chin; the heads of two others project beyond the hair, about the place of the cars; four others feem to be plaited in a knot on the upper part of the head above the wings.

" This ornament, fo placed, I fhall be able, I hope, to explain in the following paper, as the *Serpentine* or *Cherubic Diadem*, which the Egyptians, Rhodians, and fome other nations in the Eaft, placed upon the head of the divine fymbol of their God.

" Although it is reprefented in the fable of Medufa, that her fine hair became ferpents, fo transformed as a punifhment inflicted by the indignation of the Gods; yet the beauty of her countenance remained, and thus fhe is reprefented in the beft gems, which give decidedly the head of Medufa. The countenance here in this fragment is that of a bearded male, with large whifkers, not a female; of an afpect ftern, yet open as the day, Φαίδρος; τας 'ολας, juft as Mercury is defcribed in his character of Sol."[1]

The Governor then proceeds to the explanation of this mafonry, in which he difplays much ingenuity, and recondite learning; and adds the following paragraph as the general conclufion of his premifes.

1 Governor Pownal's Defcriptions and Explanations of fome Remains of Roman Antiquities, dug up in the city of Bath. Cruttwell, 1795. p. 2. 3.

" Now

" Now putting together that this *caput pinnatum*, crowned with the ferpentine diadem, was the *cherubic emblem* of the *Sun*; and that this emblem, as in its firft form was almoft univerfally placed in the fronts of the temples in Egypt, and on many in Perfia; I fay combining this idea with the fact that this city, afterwards by the Saxons called *Baden*, was originally by the Romans called *Aquæ Solis*, and facred to *Sol*; alfo with the fact, that after the time in which the Flavian family were Emperors of Rome, temples dedicated to Sol, under the theologic notions, explained in this paper, were frequently erected ; we may venture to fay *that this curious piece of antiquity is a fragment of a temple of Sol; and that this* caput pinnatum, *crowned with the ferpentine diadem, is the cherubic emblem of Sol*, placed in the front of this temple, particularly in the tympanum of the pediment."

Notwithftanding the ingenious and erudite reafoning of Governor Pownal on the fubject, I cannot but think his hypothefis is ill-founded—that the fculpture before us, fo far from being the *cherubic emblem of the Sun*, and a fragment of a temple dedicated to that Deity, is the tympanum of an edifice facred to *Minerva*, and reprefents the head of Medufa, an appropriate emblem of that Goddefs. The following obfervations will probably be thought to con-firm, or at leaft corroborate this opinion.

It may be to our purpofe to prove, in the firft place, that a temple dedicated to *Minerva*, ftood formerly in the city

city of Bath. For this fact we have the testimony of Solinus, who exprefsly tells us, a magnificent edifice of this kind was erected there by the Romans, who confidered Minerva and Apollo, as the joint tutelary Deities of its healing fprings.[1] Here fhe was probably worfhipped under her *medical character*; fince at Rome, among many other temples, fhe had one as patronefs of the Pharmaceutic Art.[2]

---

1 " Fontes in Britannia caldios," memorat (Solinus Polyhift. c. 22.)" " opiparo " excultos apparatu; quibus fontibus præful fit Minerva, in cujus æde perpetui ignes " nunquam canefcant in favillas fed ubi ignis tabuerit vertere in globos Saxeos." Quos fontes ab his aquis (Υδατα δερμα) diflinguendos non putant : ut adeo et Minervæ et Soli aquæ fuerint facratæ. Guil: Burton, Com: in Antonin: p. 260.

In the above quotation from Solinus a curious circumftance is mentioned with refpect to the *fuel confumed in the Temple of Minerva*, which, fays the writer, " is never reduced to white afhes, but converted into *ftony nodules.*" A gentleman fuggefted, that this defcription evidently pointed at *coal*, as the matter burnt in the temple of Minerva. A large heated mafs of which foffil, would produce juft what Solinus mentions; not white afhes, but roundifh, heavy cinders; not unlike in weight and appearance, a dark and porous ftone. This opinion is ftrengthened by the eafe with which coal might have been procured in the neighbourhood of this city, as it lies in almoft every direction round it, and at no great diftance from the furface. It is rendered further probable, by the certainty we have of its ufe being perfectly known to the Britons, and to the Romans alfo on their arrival here. " That the Britons in general were acquainted with this fuel, is evident from its " appellation amongft us at prefent, which is not *Saxon* but *Britifh*, and fubfifts " amongft the Irifh in their *Gual*, and amongft the Cornifh, in their *Kolan*, to this " day." Whitaker's Hift : Manchefter, v. 2. p. 37. " The Romans were as " well acquainted with our pit-coal, as with our ores and metals; in digging up " fome of the foundations of their walled city *Magna* or *Caorvarran*, 1767, coal " cinders, fome very large were turned up, glowed in the fire like other cinders, " and not to be known from them when taken out." Wallis's Hift : Northumberland, v. 1. p. 119.

2 Templi Minervæ Medicæ P, victor meminit, quod fuit in regione v. Rofin Antiq: Rom: 170.

Such

Such being the fact, and every circumſtance of the fragment before us, referring to *Minerva*, under ſome or other
of her characters, it ſeems likely that the whole belonged
originally to the temple mentioned by Solinus.

Let us, however, conſider Governor Pownal's objections
to this.

The *hair*, he obſerves, will not be found to be *crines
anguicomæ*, but, though rudely cut, to be *in its natural
ſtate*. Now, on conſidering moſt of the heads of *Meduſa*,
collected from gems, ſculptures, and coins, by antiquaries,
we find them ſtrikingly ſimilar to that under conſideration.
Hence it appears, that we are to conſider the *crinita draconibus ora*, and ſuch like expreſſions of the ancient poets
(for the antique ſculptures, after all, form the beſt com-
ment upon them), as figurative and poetical, intended to
convey the idea, that the fine hair of Meduſa was *inter-
mingled* with ſerpents ; not as exhibiting abſolutely *ſnaky
locks*, or conſiſting of ſnakes altogether.

Governor Pownal next remarks, that though the fine
hair of Meduſa became ſerpents, yet the *the beauty of her
countenance ſtill remained* ; that the face in the fragment is,
that of a *bearded male*, with *whiſkers*, and therefore cannot
be intended for the Gorgon's countenance.

Now the fact is, that Meduſa, in ancient gems and
ſculptures, is repreſented under various appearances ;
ſometimes

fometimes with a face beautiful and ferene, at others, as
convulfed with paffion, and diftorted with horror.'

The contraction of brow in the fragment, which was
intended to give an expreffion of ferocity that could not be
introduced into the eyes, agrees admirably well with the
ftern and fierce afpect generally attributed by the poets to
Medufa. On the fhield of Agamemnon fhe was to be feen
with eyes fierce, and looking horror :

Τη δ'ετι μεν Γοργω βλοσυρωπις εςεφαανωω
Δεινον δερκομενη, περι δε Δειμος τε Φοβος τε.

On that of Hercules alfo, the fame dire monfter appeared, with fimilar fearful circumftances ;

Παν δε μεταφρενον αχε καρη δεινοιο πελωρη
Γοργης·

———επι δε δεινοισι καρηνοις
Γοργειοις εδονατο μεγας Φοβος. 3

<hr/>

1 Spence's Polymetis, plate 41. fig. 2. Medufas's head, exhibiting rage and
horror, from a fhield at the foot of the ftatue of Mars, at the Borghefe Villa, near
Rome.
2 Hom : II ; xi. v. 36.
        In eo autem Gorgon trux oculis adornata erat
        Horrendum afpiciens, et circum Terrorque et fuga.
3 Heriod ΑΣΠΙΣ 'ΗΡΑΚ. v. 223. 236. omne dorfum habebat caput gravis Mon-
ftri Gorgûs—In gravibus capitibus Gorgoreis agitabatur magnus terror.

Lucan

Lucan alludes to her terrific look ,

Quos habuit vultus hamati vulnere ferri
Cæsa caput Gorgon? Quanto spiraffe veneno
Ora rear, quantumque oculos effundere mortis.[1]

A fimilar allufion occurs in Flaccus ;

——*Horrentem colubris (Ægidem), vultuque tremendam*
Gorgones.[2]

And Virgil hath not forgotten to mention *the rolling of her eyes* as a diftinguifhing and horrible circumftance in the countenance of Medufa ;

Gorgona, defecto vertentem lumina collo.[3]

That fhe is ever reprefented indeed with a beard or whifkers, I do not find. But thefe appendages may, I think, be very well accounted for, by taking into confideration that as the fculpture was intended for an elevation of thirty or forty feet, the architect might have added them (improperly enough) for the purpofes of giving more character to the countenance, and conveying into it that *mafculine ferocity*, which the poets attributed to it.[4]

1 Lib: 9. v. 680.
2 Argonau, 6. v. 176.
3 En: 8. v. 438.

4 Cupid is introduced, in Lucian's Dialogues, as telling his mother, that Minerva's appearance is fo fierce and *mafculine*, he is afraid to approach her. Δεδια ω μητερ, αιτην. Φοβερα γαρ εστι, και καροπη και δεινως ανδεικη. Tom : 1—716. The fame author tells us alfo, that a fimilar *mafculine and ferocious* look might be obferved in the *countenance of her Ægis*. P. 89.

The

The *wings* attached to the head conſtitute a further proof that *Medufa* was intended to be here repreſented. Moſt of the gems and ſculptures repreſent her with a *caput pinnatum*, which ſeems to have been thus ornamented, in alluſion to the fable of her deſtruction, accompliſhed by Perſeus with the affiſtance of Mercu,ry who accommodated the hero with his own wings, when he undertook to deſtroy this pernicious monſter.[1]

Another argument in favour of my opinion may be drawn from the ſnakes which are interwoven with the hair, particularly thoſe that are *connected together under the chin*, to which both Ovid and Virgil more eſpecially allude ;

Nexaque nodofas angue Medufa comas.
 Connexos angues.[2]

The above obſervations may, perhaps, remove the Governor's objections with reſpect to the head being that of *Medufa*.—It will now be neceſſary to notice certain ornaments obſervable on the fragment, which may be adduced as deciſive proofs of the whole referring to *Minerva* inſtead of *Sol.*

On conſidering the annexed engraving, it will be remarked that the head is ſurrounded by two circular ornaments. The external one exhibits an *olive wreath*, as is evident

from the long, narrow, and flightly indented leaves, and
the berries which accompany them.—That this tree was
facred to *Minerva*, and emblematical of her as patronefs
of the arts, is notorious.[1] In claffical mythology, fhe was
feigned to have firft prefented the valuable plant to man-
kind; and in her peaceful charaƈter, was always reprefented, either with a branch of it in her hand, or with one
encircling her helmet.[2] Another ufual accompaniment of
the fame Deity, in fculpture and gems, is the *owl*, or bird
of wifdom, which was fuppofed to be particularly agreeable
to the Goddefs of it.;

Non comes obfcurus tripodum non fulminis ardes
Veƈlor ades, flavæque fonans avis unca Minervæ.[3]

A bird of this fpecies appears on the Tympanum, juft
without the external circular ornament; which, (though
Governor Pownal confiders it as a *negative proof* of the
truth of his Hypothefis) I cannot but think, was intended as
a further indication of the exclufive claim of Minerva, to
the edifice of which it was an ornament.—The fame obfer-
vation may be made with refpeƈt to the Helmet that appears
on the oppofite fide; it being, an emblem of the *Diva
armigera*, or Minerva in her warlike charaƈter; and as
fuch, is a very common reprefentation in fculptures which

1 Olea, Minervæ fymbolum eft, cui hæc arbor facra artium habita præfes, quæ
artes ad lucernam noƈtu lucubrando nimium quantum crefcunt in qua lucerna et oleum
adhiberi folet. Ant: Auguft: Dial: in Antiq: D. 2. p. 19.

2 Id: Dial: 4. p. 69.

3 Statius, Theb: Lib: 3. v. 520.

have

have a reference to her. Though it be fomewhat defaced by the injuries of time, it ftill affords us a pretty good pattern of the Roman *Galea*; and proves how admirably this piece of Head-armour was calculated to anfwer the purpofes for which it was defigned. It might not be indeed fo light, nor perhaps, fo becoming, as the cavalry helmet of modern days: yet its conftruction rendered it much more ufeful to the wearer, and preferved him both from inconvenience and injuries, to which the imperfect form of the one now in ufe, renders him liable. The *ftrap* that appears on each fide, and which was faftened under the chin, prevented the poffibility of the helmet being thrown off in the fhock of battle, an accident that may eafily happen without fuch a precaution. This appendage was called Oχευς, and made a part of the ancient Grecian, as well as Roman Helmet.[r] Another fuperiority which the Roman Head-armour poffeffed over the modern one, was the *buccula* or leathern flap, that depended from the back of the helmet, and covered the neck and part of the fhoulders. This addition muft, doubtlefs, have been fomewhat incommodious to the wearer, until ufe had reconciled him to it; but the inconvenience was amply recompenfed by its utility, fince it preferved thofe parts from being wounded, which being left expofed by the modern Cafque, are, as I am informed, very frequently, and feverely injured.

r It was this ftrap, which, had it not been for the interpofition of Venus, would have been the death of Paris, in his conteft with Menelaus.

Αγχι δε μιν πολεμιτος ιμας απαλης υπο δειρης,

Ο, ν τ' αφθς ενο εγνη, τ τατο τετραφατων.   Hom. l. γ. 371.

I pro

I proceed now to the laſt, perhaps the ſtrongeſt proof, that the Tympanum under conſideration may be conſidered as part of the temple of Minerva mentioned by Solinus.— It is well known that the ancients eſteemed certain *beaſts* to be particularly agreeable to particular Gods.—Theſe, on feſtivals, and other ſolemn occaſions, they offered up ; and each Deity was regaled with the favor that aroſe from the ſacrifice of his favorite animal;

Κνισση δ'ερανον ικεν ελισσομενη περι καπνω. [1]

It is equally certain, that the Goddeſs *Minerva* was thought to prefer an *Heifer of a year old* to any other beaſt; and, under this abſurd impreſſion, the ancients frequently made that offering to her, as the moſt grateful one in their power.—Such a ſacrifice does *Diomed* promiſe to *Minerva*, as the recompence of her aſſiſtance in an expedition he is about to undertake;

Σοι δ'αυ εγω ρεξω βυν ηνιν, ευρυμετωπον,
Αδμητην, ην ουπω υπο ζυγον ηγαγεν ανηρ·
Την τοι εγω ρεξω, χρυσον κερασιν περιχευας [2]

And Helenus adviſes twelve of them to be ſacrificed to the ſame Goddeſs, as the moſt likely means of engaging her compaſſion in behalf of Troy and its inhabitants;

1 Hom': II: 1. v. 317. Nidor autem ad cælum ibat circumfuſus fumo.
2 II: x. v. 292.

Και

Και οι υπασχεσθαι δυσκαιδεκα βας εν ταις,
Ηνις, ηκεςας ιεςευταμεν, ' &c.

Now it is a curious and remarkable circumstance, strongly corroborative of the opinion I have ventured to suggest, that *several horns,* together with parts of *skulls,* which from their shape, figure, and size, are, unquestionably, those of *yearlings,* were found on the same spot with the Tympanum and other fragments of the temple to which it belonged. This fact seems to settle, beyond doubt, that the *customary* sacrifices to Minerva had been offered in this edifice; and, when connected with the other circumstances above adduced, forms so powerful a body of *presumptive proof* that the edifice itself was consecrated to this Goddess, as nothing, but absolute demonstration to the contrary, can resist or overturn.[2]

  1 Et ei voveat duodecim boves in templo
    Anniculas, jugum non paffas, facrificaturum, &c.   Il : 6. v. 93.

  2 The other fragment herewith reprefented, is part of a *flying Genius*; two of which appear to have fupported the outer wreath, as may be concluded from the remaining hands and arm vifible on the right fide of it.

www.ingramcontent.com/pod-product-compliance
Lightning Source LLC
Chambersburg PA
CBHW030604270326
41927CB00007B/1034